# WELLSPRING

# Wellspring

## A Story from the Deep Country

Barbara Dean

Illustrations by Julie Miyasaki

ISLAND PRESS, COVELO, CALIFORNIA

Printed in the United States of America

Thanks to Peter, Lois, Taya, Sheila, Michael, Ardie, Jim, Twink, Paul, Tania,
and Cathy, in addition to those whose names appear on these pages, all of whom
have their own versions of these and other stories; and to all of the above and the
whole extended family, especially Joan, for advice and support along the way.
Special thanks to Twink for endless typing, Jeremy for careful editing,
Diana for the front cover, and Russell Fuller for the back cover photograph.

Library of Congress Cataloging in Publication Data

Dean, Barbara, 1946 —
Wellspring, a story from the deep country.
1. Country life — California.  2. Collective settlements — California.  I. Title.
HT421.D4      979.4      79-2606
ISBN 0-933280-01-7

*For my parents,*
*Ben and Margaret Dean,*
*and for Kathy*

# Preface

*World without and world within, after all, whether one knows it or not, are expressions of one another; interdependent and ceaselessly in communication, serving something greater than the sum of themselves.*

— LAURENS VAN DER POST

WELLSPRING is the story of my life with fifteen friends on a square mile of beautiful, isolated land in northern California. When we came here together in 1971, we told our parents that we intended to start an alternative school; we told each other that we wanted to do something different with our lives; I told myself that I wanted to discover who I really was. Eight years later, the ranch has become home. Our lives together defy easy categorization — but clearly the ranch is the "something different" each of us was seeking.

Jung tells us that the choices we make in life must necessarily leave something else unchosen. If, in choosing a course, we reject the reality of our alternatives, we may also fail to recognize the importance of the rejected course to our lives. Jung predicts that we cannot become whole as individuals or as civilizations without welcoming these shadows, these roads not taken, to the light of our understanding.

The choices I have made for my life are, in a sense, the shadow of the dominant culture of twentieth-century America. I live alone in a yurt built from this land, by my hands — not the chosen setting or style of many people. And yet I find these choices to be the logical culmination of how I was raised: the values my parents gave me have led here, to this lovely, windswept meadow. Though the trappings of their life and mine are quite different, the essential purposes and qualities are the same. And it is out of a sense of that deep sameness that I have wanted to write this book.

Living on the land has restored to me a feeling of wonder that I knew as a child. My consuming purpose is to pursue that wonder, to realize God. I would not have phrased it that way eight years ago; then I would have said I wanted to find personal meaning or truth. But no matter what the words, they describe the same yearning for an answer to the mystery of life that people have sought in every place and in every time. In that search and in that yearning, especially, I am no different from anyone else.

What is different about my life is simply where and how it transpires, and that is the subject of these pages. Since we live far from the entertainments of the city, storytelling takes the place of television and movies for us. After a day's work, we gather at dinner to tell of the animals we encountered, the machines that didn't work, and the random thoughts that occurred to us. From these daily exchanges, some stories linger to be told again. By the third or fourth telling, they have a shape of their own and a truth that is larger than the original incident. Sharing stories is a way of connecting with each other; I offer these stories from my life to illuminate some of the shadows and the choices in all of our lives.

A wellspring is where water bubbles forth from the earth, a source of continual supply. The land, for me, is a wellspring of pure delight. I simply love living here. The quiet joy that I feel as I watch dawn spread over the meadow has only intensified in these eight years, and I can't imagine that it could ever dim. I understand now that I was drawn here by an urge much deeper than the desire to start an alternative school. I am here because it is where I belong. This is where, for me, the world without and the world within become one, and I am pulled resolutely toward God. And that, of course, is the only story there is.

*June 1979*
*Covelo, California*

# Contents

# I
# Point of Departure

THE shrill, unearthly cry silenced our chatter. The sound rebounded off the distant hills, echoed across the windswept meadow, and pursued us down the long, dusty driveway. As we pulled up in front of the tattered log house, it came again: "Aaaeeeooowww!! Aaaeeeooowww!!" To my uninitiated ears, the sound was like the scream of a child in pain.

Annie came across the lawn to greet us. She didn't seem especially disturbed. "Didn't you hear that?" I asked incredulously.

The cry erupted once again, piercing the warm May sunshine.

"Oh, that?" Annie grinned, obviously enjoying my dismay. "That's a peacock. There are twelve of them and they're better than watchdogs."

Peacocks?! Somehow the extraordinary presence of holy birds from Southeast Asia roaming wild in this northern California countryside made me realize a fact I'd overlooked in the previous months of planning. Suddenly I knew that my life was about to change dramatically. As I slammed the car door, the peacock called out once more, and I felt a tingle of anticipation. That cry is so linked with my memory of the beginning that hearing it still brings forth all the excitement, the apprehension, and the anguish of those first few months.

Eight of us tumbled out of the old Volkswagen bus, stomachs queasy from the long mountain road, and spread ourselves on the grass in front of the log house. My mental pictures of those first moments are hazy, but I remember how I felt as clearly as if it were today. I was awestruck, not so much by the beauty, which in retrospect seems to have grown on me slowly, but by the presence of the land. To think of buying the meadow that stretched forever before us: it was presumption that made my head spin.

I glanced at the other faces alongside mine, wondering if my feelings were shared. Susie, alert and fresh as ever, was already tending to business at hand — screwing the nipple on a freshly filled bottle for six-month-old T. A. Kathleen, whose dark-haired beauty was a little green from the road, lay staring at the sky, while her daughter Josie, three, asked for a glass of orange juice, now please. Russell offered her a sip from his just-opened beer instead.

Next to Russell, Deborah examined a flower which Kristine, her five-year-old daughter, brought; their long blond hair melted together in the late afternoon sun. Ranger, Annie, and Ashley, the advance scouting crew who had flown here the week before in Ashley's little plane, looked brown and satisfied. If they had ever experienced the disorientation I felt now, a few days on the land had transformed it into giggling triumph.

Missing that afternoon were Bruce, Mark, Carol, and Michael. Most of us had never met Mark and Carol, friends of Ashley from high school. Susie, Ashley, Russell, Michael, and Bruce had been my college classmates at Duke, but our acquaintance there was superficial, and I hadn't expected to see any of them after graduation. Then after a year of teaching in New York City, I drove to California with a Duke friend who reintroduced me to Russell. By fall, he and I founded an alternative school, Rivendell, for three- to eight-year-olds in Palo Alto. A month later he fell in love with Deborah, mother of one of our students, Kristine.

[ 2 ]

For two years we struggled with the common dilemmas of alternative schools — uncertain funding, parental dissension, shaky noncurriculum. In the fall of the second year, Debby left her public school job to help out with Rivendell, and Michael left UCLA graduate school to join us for the second semester. By spring, after a field trip to Mexico with fifteen children and six adults in three VW buses, we were certain that Rivendell would survive and continue to be a solid alternative to the local public schools.

But by then I also knew I needed to do something else. Despite my high hopes and near-total freedom to set up the school as I chose, Rivendell didn't satisfy my desire to really make a difference. We had created a humane alternative to the public school system, but was it a real learning environment? It didn't seem so to me. Still we adults set the pace, and we used various ruses to trick the children into learning. I wanted to find a place where — as I phrased it at the time — learning would be fun and spontaneous, where living and learning would happen together, naturally.

I began to pay more attention to the talk that was occupying most of the time I spent with Russell, Michael, and Debby. They were about to act on a dream that Ash, Susie, Michael, and Russell had conceived around the bridge table at Duke years before: a dream of buying some land in the country and starting a school. One day I caught myself saying "we" instead of "you" and I realized that I was going to do it too. I remember no real decision, and that alone should have alerted me to the significance this step was going to assume in my life. I can spend hours weighing the pros and cons of a blue shirt or a white one, but all the truly important choices in my life have happened without my noticing.

After graduating from Duke, Ash and Susie were married, and then Ash was drafted into the army. In Germany, where he was stationed, they met Ranger and Annie, another couple trying to survive army life abroad. By the time I joined the group, Ranger and Annie had decided to join, too. Bruce and Kathy, who had also been married after college, had kept in touch with the group through letters while Bruce worked first for IBM in New York, and then for a radical newspaper in North Carolina.

The plan was that everyone would gather in Palo Alto in May, 1971. We would spend the summer getting to know each other, while we considered where would be our best chance to find land. We wanted a piece that we could buy outright, with money Susie and Annie had inherited, probably about eighty acres. No one really expected to be able to afford anything in California.

That was the plan. What happened was that Ashley, once he had arrived in Palo Alto, quickly tired of waiting for Russell, Deb, Michael, and me to finish the school year, and decided to look around the California countryside with Ranger and Annie to learn the real estate game. A few days after they headed north, the rest of us in Palo Alto received a postcard from a little town no one had ever heard of. "Come," the card said. "We think you'll like this."

And so here we were, spread out on an unfamiliar hillside: upper- and middle-class kids, altered forever by the sixties; sports heroes and Phi Betes, hoping to change the world; a bunch of scruffy hippies, thinking of buying some real estate.

That first afternoon we wandered around trying to take stock. There were 670 acres, two functioning houses, thirty head of cattle, a D7 Caterpillar. It was almost out of the question financially, definitely out of the realm of our carefully-thought-out plans. We set up a volleyball net in the meadow, and in an effort to merge the familiar with the strange, played volleyball for hours. At dusk we ate spaghetti cooked over an open fire and settled down to talk.

The land was beautiful, we agreed. It had plenty of water and two houses already habitable to get us started. Lots of potential. But how would we raise the money? Were we capable of running a ranch of this size? Were we even sure we wanted to live together?

During the previous months, when letters had been the only means of communicating, some critical differences of opinion had emerged. We hadn't agreed on the kind of community we wanted to have, how we would make decisions, deal with money, or add new members to the group. The point of spending the summer together before we bought land was precisely to allow us to work out those questions. And now here we were, doing things absolutely backwards.

Ranger wanted the land to be open to anyone who came. Ashley objected strenuously, wanting to choose the people he would raise his children with. Russell wanted Annie and Susie to liquidate all their stock investments or put them under the control of the group. Susie and Annie said no, that felt like unfair group pressure. Ranger and I favored decision making by consensus; Ashley doubted whether that was practical and suggested that we stick to majority rule. Debby pointed out that we hadn't even met Mark and Carol yet; how could we possibly know whether or not we wanted to live with them? And with what authority had Ashley invited them, without asking the rest of the group?

The glow from the fire illuminated the increasing tension in our faces as it became clear that we had many more questions than we could answer. Disagreements that had surfaced in letters became sharp in the cool night air, and the pressure to come to a decision on buying land while

[ 5 ]

so many important questions remained unresolved made both patience and understanding seem irrelevant. Voices became hoarse and tight. Our little campfire circle grew more and more removed from the harmony of the meadow.

Finally Annie announced that she was going to sleep, and she unrolled her sleeping bag and climbed in. That seemed the only way out of a disturbing evening and in uncharacteristic unanimity, we all did the same. I drifted into a troubled sleep feeling very insignificant under more stars than I had ever seen in the Palo Alto sky.

The next day we went to the river.

The river is one of the nation's last truly wild and natural waterways. It lies alongside the eastern boundary of the land, just far enough away to transform getting there into a pilgrimage. The real estate agent who showed Ashley the land never mentioned it, a remarkable oversight that nearly cost him his sale. But his omission allowed us to discover it for ourselves, which was as it should have been.

Ashley led the way, through the rolling, flower-filled meadows, down the forest slopes on paths blazed by deer, across creeks strewn with moss-covered rocks and loud with little waterfalls. Then the forest opened out into a gorge, and eleven of us stood dwarfed by the boulders — pink, green, and red — that lay scattered along the river's edge. We looked into the water, clean enough to drink and so clear that we could see brightly colored water snakes gliding near the bottom. We looked at each other. Then our clothes were at our feet, and we were in the cool water, feeling the pull of the current on our city-tender skin. All our rational arguments of the night before — "But it's too much land" — "How will we ever pay for it?" — "But we don't even know each other yet!" — were forgotten as we body-surfed through the rapids and stretched on the sun-warmed rocks, listening to the surge of water moving swiftly toward the sea.

We played together and swam for hours. When the time came to head up the hill and prepare for the long journey back to the city, hardly a word was spoken. No one wanted to reopen the discussion of the night before. I think that the decision had already been made by then, but most of us hardly dared admit it to ourselves. Deciding to take the plunge, to jump straight into the unknown and buy this 670 acres, contradicted every principle by which most of us had directed our lives until then. To buy a square mile of remote, abandoned land, an hour's drive over mountain roads from the nearest store, two hours from the nearest hospital, and not a farmer or a mechanic or a nurse in the group; to make a down payment with only fuzzy ideas of where the rest of the money would come from: by any rational standard, it was sheer lunacy.

But there are other forces loose in the universe than reason, and the pull of those other forces — forces of nature, destiny, love — was strong enough to undermine reason's stranglehold on our lives. By the time we reached Palo Alto that evening, we were talking about "our" land.

We spent the next week trying, unsuccessfully, to rationalize the decision. The following weekend we signed the papers. Then school was out, and we moved to the country.

We were the original city slickers. The first country people we had dealings with saw us coming miles away.

During the week between the time we signed the papers and the day we moved up to the land, while we were still in Palo Alto finishing school and tying up loose ends, Susie found an ad in the paper for horses for sale or trade. Horses! We wanted horses; many of us were riders and had expectations of long, happy hours riding over our land. We called the number listed in the ad and went to see the horses after school the next day.

Bruce drove the VW bus with ten of us, seven adults and three children inside, from Palo Alto to a dusty road near San Jose. We were all a little giddy with excitement and self-importance. The trip south was filled with discussion of what kinds of horses we wanted and what kind of bargain we would drive, and speculation about what manner of folks we would be bargaining with. By the time we arrived, we were expecting Scarlett O'Hara and Rhett Butler, at least — and, sure enough, we found them, vintage 1971!

The cowhand who met us at the gate was the foreman, meaning he ran the ranch for the gentleman and his lady. The gentleman was getting out of the horse business and moving into cattle, the foreman explained, and wanted to sell these horses or trade them for cattle. "Perfect," Bruce replied. "We've just bought a ranch with thirty head of cattle, and we'd like to trade them for horses."

The cowhand hid his smile and went into the house to get the gentleman's lady.

We liked her right away. Slim, long-legged, wearing Levi's, cowboy boots, and a cowboy hat, she lit her cigarette by striking a match on her pant leg. She was fancy in the way I imagined a ranch-bred lady would be, and her talk was at the same time conspiratorial with us and loyal to her man, laced with what we assumed was ranching slang and not a few obscenities.

She told the cowhand which horses to bring us, and told us their histories as he brought them around. "This one we bought at an auction in

Colorado. Racing blood, but he'd been handled badly. Jim's worked with him hard, till he sets up real nice now. That one is my favorite; hate to part with her, but Jim says they all have to go." And so on.

We took turns riding. Bruce landed in the ankle-deep dust seconds after he hopped on the back of a nice-looking palomino mare.

"Quirky saddle," the cowhand explained, and fiddled with the cinch. Michael climbed on next and found himself the star of a spectacular bucking bronco performance, to the accompaniment of enthusiastic cheers from the sidelines. Finally he managed to jump safely to the ground, and the horse, by now wet with sweat and frothing at the mouth, stood panting in the center of the ring.

"Well, she's a temperamental one, doesn't like men," the lady said. "Put a gal on her back and she's as fine a horse as you'll ever see; lots of spirit, too." Bruce mumbled something about wasn't it a little late to tell us that, and Michael, still trying to catch his breath, suggested that maybe one of the "gals" should have a try.

Annie hesitated only a minute. She eased herself onto the broad golden back, and Apple Juice (as we later named her), whether because she was simply tired of all the commotion or because she really did dislike men, let her stay. Annie and Apple Juice walked and trotted five full rounds of the corral. We "gals" wanted to buy her on the spot.

There were more horses to try out. Bruce had better luck with a huge brown gelding, who clearly wanted to please; Debby found a wild-looking Appaloosa who pranced prettily around the ring. When my turn came, I settled for a few circles on an old brown mare who didn't look too interested in keeping her head off the ground, much less in getting me off her back.

We talked terms. What kind of cattle did we have? "Polled Herefords," Debby answered (glad we had looked up the meaning of polled and the pronunciation of Hereford in the dictionary the night before). How many did we want to trade? The terms of our mortgage contract said we could sell no more than six. How about six horses for six steer? I nearly fell off the fence. Privately we'd figured the most we could get for six steer would be two, maybe three horses. We never suspected that six of our healthy, range-fed Herefords were easily worth fifteen of their horses at the current prices. "Well, sure, that sounds all right," Michael said, trying to sound like we were thinking it over.

We chose the horses. Jim and cowhand were to drive up with them in three weeks; they'd look over the cattle then, and if they liked the steers, they'd trade us horses for cattle on the spot. Done, we said, and sped up the dusty road in our little VW bus, thinking we'd made a killing. I'm sure cowhand, Jim, and ranch-bred lady *knew* they had.

Three weeks later up drove Jim, cowhand, and six horses. This road is not easy to negotiate in anything larger than a three-quarter-ton pickup; Jim and cowhand looked a little frayed from getting their truck and a six-horse trailer around the mountain curves. But despite the heat, the effort, and the dust, their grins returned when they saw us. They asked for water, took a look at the cattle, who were conveniently gathered at the head of the meadow, and nodded to each other. We wanted to unload the horses.

We'd all been looking forward to this day. The horses were a missing piece in our dream puzzle of life on a ranch. Jim and cowhand lowered the ramp of the trailer. "They're a little tuckered out from the trip, of course," they warned.

We were learning that country people speak in understatement. One by dusty one, the horses stumbled out of the trailer, "tuckered out by the trip" to say the least. Struggling to reconcile our memory of the horses we'd chosen with the sorry beasts before us, we urged them toward the rich meadow grass, hoping that a little good grazing might rekindle some spark of life.

But there were only five. I looked in the trailer. One horse remained, apparently unable to move. Jim said he was a little bit under the weather but with a good night's rest and some feed, he'd perk right up and be the best of the lot. Jim and cowhand half pushed, half carried Horse A (as we have called him since) out of the trailer. We watched. "That horse is dead," Russell said. "Oh, no," Jim said, with a patronizing air that won us over, "just you wait until morning. He'll perk right up."

It occurred to us that we should cover ourselves just in case. Michael drew up a contract that made the whole deal hinge on the health of all six horses, so that if any one of them failed to "perk right up," we were released from any obligation. It turned out that Jim didn't care much about the technicalities; he wasn't going to be able to take the cattle with him that trip anyway, and, sure, he'd give us three weeks to get to know the horses, and then he'd be back up to finalize the deal. He and cowhand drove away, back down that long, hot, dusty road, with an empty trailer, within the hour. They left their names and address, promising to get in touch.

We had six tired horses. By early the next morning, Horse A was on the ground, unable to rise. An hour later, as we watched in near disbelief, he went into spectacular feet-in-the-air convulsions, and then he was dead. Ranger used the D7 Caterpillar we had bought with the land to bury him. One of our neighbors, the foreman of a 30,000-acre horse and cattle ranch to the north, happened to be there to witness the final seizures. "Looks like sleeping sickness to me," he said. "You had the horse vet-checked?"

Well, no, we hadn't exactly. Sleeping sickness. Was that serious?

It was serious. An epidemic of a new strain of encephalitis was sweeping the country, but it hadn't been in our area. Yet. The vet confirmed the cause of death and gave us and all the neighbors serum to protect the rest of the horses. For our neighbors up the road, that meant a round-up of major proportions, a loss of several working days, and considerable expense for the vaccine. We were off to a great start in neighborly relations.

Apple Juice tried to attack the horseshoer when he touched her rear feet. "That horse is a killer. I can see it in her eyes," he said. We didn't argue.

Pumpkin had calcium deposits in his feet. The kids had a great time walking him around the meadow, until he became too lame even for that. Big Dude, the gentle gelding Bruce liked, developed a permanently lame foreleg, and we never got to know Horse E very well because he had an unpleasant habit of taking off at a full gallop when anyone got near him. Of the six, only Goose, the wild-looking Appaloosa, proved ridable. We wrote to Jim, told him the deal was off because of Horse A's death, and asked him to come and collect his herd. As we discovered later, we were not the first to have had trouble with Jim's business deals. He asked no questions, just said he was eager to get his affairs in order because he was on his way to Mexico. He arrived within the week with an empty trailer. Mark bought Goose for $150, tack thrown in gratis; Jim loaded the remaining four horses into the trailer, and then he disappeared forever down the dusty road.

The horse deal was not the only time our city colors showed. Mistakes were inevitable as we college grads, with degrees in such useful disciplines as French and history, settled in to fix the tractor and plant the garden, book in one hand, tool in the other. The neighbors (who, to our immense relief, were genuinely courteous and forgiving about our sleeping sickness blunder) contributed helping hands and words of advice, and laughed with us at our ignorance of country ways. We asked Andy, our closest neighbor down the road, when we could expect the first frost. He looked at us with a steady eye. "Well," he said, in no hurry to get the words out, "I'd say you could expect it 'bout the time the thermometer hits 32 degrees."

As the sun was making heat rise in ripples from the meadow, we scrubbed and painted the houses; planted an acre of vegetables and put a fence around it; repaired and maintained the tractor, truck, and cars; learned how to cut and brand our Hereford cattle; put in an irrigation system to the garden; took out the kinks in the house plumbing. We learned enough plumbing, gardening, vet care, mechanics, and general troubleshooting to make it. We did it mostly with our bare hands, and felt a degree of fulfillment we had not known in our previous, more cerebral occupations. Sitting down to a meal of home-grown zucchini and salad with home-baked bread was a real and tangible satisfaction. Afterward, Ranger would take out his guitar and we'd sing into the cool summer nights, our voices mingling with those of the frogs until all earthly sounds dissolved in the murmur of the stars.

But my memories of the first summer are not so much of what we did as of how it felt. No words can come close to conveying how it really was to live it: the tingling feeling of electricity in the air at sunrise, the exhilaration of working together all day long, the raucous sense of celebration with which we sat down to supper together each evening. Nor is it possible to describe the wildness that filled me with longing, the explosion of feelings long hidden, unleashed in this paradise apparently without law. Emotions and passions which seemed as new and strange as the wilderness itself took us over, and in days that lasted for years apiece, proceeded to play havoc with our "civilized" sense of propriety.

Now that I have met a number of other people who have made the move from city to country, I realize that the transition is possible to manage with families, sanity, and basic value systems intact. But for us moving to the land meant a radical departure from everything we'd previously known. We were determined to do something entirely new, and insisted on figuring everything out for ourselves. What we didn't consciously leave behind, the events of the first summer did away with.

I know now that — given those internal compulsions — nothing we might have done to "prepare" ourselves could have softened the blow that actually moving inflicted on our psyches; in the light of what happened in the first months, the disagreements we had around the campfire that first weekend seem ludicrously mild. At Rivendell I had seen the uncomfortable period of transition when a public school child enters an environment where, suddenly, all the cues she has come to seek as an index to behavior simply aren't there. The tumult we experienced that summer, both individually and collectively, made me understand that chaos from the inside.

We were in a similar situation, placed in a strange and demanding environment, where a lifetime of learned behavior wasn't enough. Even our basic survival — growing food, getting fuel, making shelter — depended on skills we didn't have, and there were no bookstores, movies, or other friends to turn to when the going got rough. Simply every familiar element in our lives had changed, and we who had learned so well to read the cues in the world out there were like bus drivers trying to steer by the stars.

The shock precipitated changes that might have taken years to unfold in a more structured, controlled situation. We found ourselves questioning basic values, found that some of us didn't really want the things we had always thought we wanted. And we found that we really didn't know each other or ourselves very well at all.

The upheaval in personal relationships dealt the deepest blows. Ranger and Annie split apart that first summer; in the year that followed, Mark and Carol, Ash and Susie, and Russell and Debby separated. Bruce and Kathy, who had been most independent of each other of all the couples from the beginning, lived together on and off. As a single person, I did not have to face the pain of separating from someone I had been married to for years, but I fast became personally involved in the violent and conflicting emotions that swirled about us all.

Perhaps hardest of all was trying to figure out *why*. Why was this happening? What were we doing wrong? Was it an inevitable part of communal living, or was it a reaction to the other tensions we were experiencing? Many of the relationships were already in trouble when we arrived; would they have fallen apart in time anyway? Did the move to the land only speed the process? Were the marriage bonds too fragile, too lightly made to stand up to the complexity of group living in the stark light of survival on the land? Or did the first separation start a horrible, accidental chain reaction?

It's impossible to know; we've hypothesized endlessly. In retrospect it does not seem surprising that personal relationships would be affected by a life change that was so abrupt and cataclysmic, but the pain that surfaced then has taken years to heal. We tried to handle it with a sense of the absurd and a growing facility for black humor, but in the end each one of us had to meet the painful realities in a solitude that was deeper and darker than we'd ever known.

And we argued. The sorrow and uncertainty that assailed each one of us erupted in endless and destructive discussions on everything from the morality of buying paper towels to the politics of monogamy. It didn't take long to discover that most of our ideas were miles apart — and those late summer meetings became the forum for our individual desperate attempts to hold on to some vestige of shaken self-images.

By the end of the first summer, I felt bereft, somewhat against my conscious wishes — not only of the patterns I had wanted to leave behind, but also of some ways of thinking and behaving that I wasn't ready to relinquish gracefully. That process, which had seemed so romantically exciting in May, by September often felt just plain *hard*.

But then something happened that showed me how much I had changed, in spite of myself. One morning at the tail end of summer, the day of the first fall rains, we were gathered at the White House to clear up a meeting of the night before. That meeting had been about whether or not we should make a float for the Labor Day parade in town, and it was one of those issues that separated us along lines of politics and style. Should we invest our time and money in such a project when money was short, winter was near, and our contribution might not be welcomed anyway? The day was cold and gray, as we were, and the White House felt dank and dreary.

Suddenly Carol noticed a most unlikely spectacle: two figures, followed by a huge pinto horse laden with burlap bags, walking across the meadow. We are not conveniently located for visitors to arrive by foot; this incident remains one of a very few of its kind to date. We had become accustomed to the unexpected that summer, but as the figures came closer into view, our jaws fell, one after another.

The short one was Bill, an old man with a wife or two and unnumbered children back in Sacramento; he'd been on the road most of his life. The other, the one who was leading the pinto, was Tony. Tony looked about twenty-eight. He wore a fringed buckskin vest, a handsome fur jacket, and high leather boots. His hair was a deep brown to match his eyes, and it hung to his shoulders. Around his neck were fifteen or twenty strands of love beads, the kind you can buy in quantity at a craft store and string yourself.

Tony and Bill were on their way to Canada by foot, to seek their fortunes and live the good life in the fine mountain man tradition. As the days passed, the life we were living looked pretty good to Bill, and he stayed here for a couple of months. Tony and the big pinto horse went on to the northlands alone, after a week with us.

Bill lent a hand in the garden, the sink, or wherever needed, but Tony spent most of his time at the kitchen table, stocking up for harder days ahead, no doubt. He called us all brothers and sisters and talked a lot about love and sharing. Before Tony left, he took each one of us aside, looked deep into our eyes, and moved one strand of love beads from his neck to ours. It was the kind of harmless little ritual I used to like.

But now, instead of returning Tony's meaningful gaze, as I probably would have done three months earlier, I squirmed. A summer on the land had made the love he preached seem thin and artificial. Suddenly I saw in him the reflection of the soulless, mass-produced image of ourselves that I knew by then would never be equal to the demands of this real life. I felt a flash of defiance toward all that brother-sister, back-to-the-land rhetoric — and caught a glimpse of the toughness of spirit I would need to shake off my remaining preconceptions and get down to the business of finding out what life and I were all about.

Clearly the blind leap of faith that first day at the river wasn't enough. I had to be willing to open myself to the challenges that this leap implied.

From somewhere the dedication and strength have come to do just that. Everyone who went through the first summer is still an active member of the family. In the face of broken relationships, financial insecurity, and daily chaos, that says something about the power of the dream.

But that day at the end of summer when Tony bestowed us all with love beads, none of us knew for certain that we would still be here in five years. All I knew, as I submitted to his ceremony, was that life was not the way Tony wanted it to be. Fifteen strands of beads lighter, Tony packed several loaves of homemade bread in his knapsack and led his beautiful pinto into the sunset. I watched him fade away, an appropriate mirage for our first summer on the land.

# II

# The Meadow
# Is My Mantra

IN THOSE hot, tumultuous summer days when everyone seemed to be going crazy at once, I started taking long walks through the land to clear my head. I wanted answers to the conflicts that were tearing me apart and peace for the turmoil raging inside. I returned not with answers, but with the calming glimpse of a world beyond my human confusion. I was drawn powerfully to the land, to the wordless presence of nature. I felt in the hills a wisdom I hungered for, heard in the wind the whisper of something larger than myself. Something connected deep within me, and I suddenly knew why I was here.

As I walked on the crest of the meadow, my heartbeat quickened and I felt a renewal of a relationship with nature I had enjoyed as a child, and that seemed to come from deep in my bones and spirit even then. When I was young, I loved nothing more than to roam in the fields and groves of trees that surrounded my home; the trees and grasses were soulmates, very personal company in a happy childhood that also included lively human friends. I have spent long stretches of my life since then away from nature: four years of college, a year in New York City, two years in Palo Alto. They were happy and successful years by most measures, but always colored by a nagging sense of exile that would disappear only on a windy hilltop or near a sparkling stream.

But now, finally, I was home — in the arms of nature. I felt again that deep sense of belonging that I had associated only with the innocent security of childhood. Once again I felt a part of the world; unquestioning, unquestionable peace and certainty of welcome flooded me. That feeling is growing still. I can stand alone at the edge of the meadow, watching the shadowed tips of the fir trees on the distant hill tickle the edges of a star-strewn sky, shivering as the lonely wail of a coyote rises from the river gorge and splits the night in halves — and feel completely, totally, at home and at ease with the universe.

Here I watch the light change from dawn to darkness and back to light. I watch the moon grow and diminish and return again. The seasons change, the clouds move, the mists rise. The land frames my life and gives me substance and bedrock on which to grow. The meadow is my mantra, my womb. The forest holds me in its shadow; it is dark, mysterious, tangled.

This land, and the rocks, trees, plants, and animals that share it with me, are active participants in my life. They are personal friends, with whom my moods and emotions seem to interact. I cannot explain this, nor do I want to: I can only affirm that it is so. One cannot live close to nature for very long without becoming aware of the real and deep correspondence between all living things, a correlation in thought, emotion, and happening that is too perfect and frequent to be written off as pure coincidence. The land and its inhabitants are as real and active and individually unique to me as they have been to every people everywhere who have lived close to nature.

This land has a personality of its own. The hills (mountains, really — part of the Coast Range) were formed about 30 million years ago, which makes them still young as mountains go. The Appalachians, for example, are closer to 600 million years of age. This land is 2,000 feet above sea level; the highest mountains we can see are 6,000 feet. The hills give the land its character; it is steep, sharp, abrupt. From the air, the ranch looks like a lopsided shelf, hanging out in space, one foot off the edge. It is all angles, acute and cockeyed, lapped together like a jigsaw puzzle that doesn't quite fit.

The rocks that are scattered everywhere — in the middle of meadows, on forested slopes, in the riverbed — are lightly metamorphic, the product of a period of high pressure and low temperature. The pressure came about too abruptly for the elements to be well sorted, resulting in rocks that are an amazing jumble of color — blue, orange, green, red — and lined with twists and turns that show the pattern of their formation. Generally rough-hewn, the rocks are still subject to shaping by the weather and the river and to grinding by the movement of the earth. The whole area is young geologically, actively changing even now.

Natural vegetation is a mixture of coniferous forest, oak woodland, and a touch of chapparal. Primary forest growth is dominated by Douglas fir, blended with several varieties of oak; two or three different kinds of pine, alder, madrone, bay laurel (pepperwood to the old-timers), and maple. The ranch was logged ten years before we bought it, and the removal of nearly all the large fir trees from that natural blend has greatly changed the character of the forest. Manzanita is everywhere, starting the cycle of second growth. Because of the logging, the light now reaches the forest floor and nourishes a wide variety of green plants that would have remained dormant otherwise.

The logging has left its mark. This land is a sad example of careless logging practices; the cutting here was done sloppily, and, in betrayal of nature's generosity, with no thought of giving back something for what was taken away. There are huge fir logs lying many places in the woods, trees that were cut and then left because the center was soft, because they were found to be a few inches too small after they'd been felled, or because they didn't fit on the truck that day. Slash — trees and bushes uprooted and tossed aside in order to make roads for trucks and bulldozers, trees and branches caught in the way of a falling tree, and small trees dead from windfall after the larger trees which buffered the wind were taken out — was everywhere when we bought the land, as were the logging roads, the dead and forgotten machinery, and the beer cans. We have cleaned up what we can, but the scars remain.

As I walk over the land, I remember the Indian belief that everything that has ever happened in a place is there still. In the forest, images of loggers loom before me, and I can almost hear the chain saws, the Caterpillars, the crash of falling trees. Around the houses and in the once-cultivated meadows I feel the presence of the pioneers who were probably the first to claim ownership of the land and with that ownership the right to kill and chase away the native people who made their homes there and the right to cut into the earth and change the course of the streams.

The spirit of the Indian is strong here, too, woven in the grasses and flowing with the river. We found a stone mortar and pestle underneath an oak tree near the orchard, and arrowheads frequently turn up in the garden turf. I think this must have been a rich life for the Indians who lived here. The vegetation provides nuts, berries, greens, and herbs. And animals — deer, squirrel, fish — also abound. What I know of Indian life and what I feel from the hills, which seem still to echo their voices, is in sharp contast to what I have seen of the white man's ways. My heart responds to the way the Indian apparently lived; I, too, want to live *with* the land rather than *on* it; I want to learn the give and take of nature so that my life will reflect the unity that I know exists.

When we finally stopped talking around the campfire that first strange weekend, when we were still wondering whether or not to buy, we all slept outside at the head of the meadow. I awoke suddenly just before dawn to see our little circle surrounded by thirty pairs of large brown eyes. Startled, I stared hard into the semi-darkness, wondering what creatures the eyes belonged to. And then I made out the forms of the Hereford cattle that had roamed the land unattended since their owners moved away six years before. They had not seen humans for those six years, and they must have been astonished to find us lying in *their* meadow. As dawn eased across the sky, I could imagine what the mothers were saying to their calves, who had never seen such strange animals, and I wondered how the old heifers felt about coming into contact with people again. The eyes gave nothing away, but I felt distinctly uncomfortable under their steady gaze. Clearly, we were the intruders.

Images of the pioneers flashed across my mind, and I wanted to apologize to the cattle for all those buffalo. But how could I? I, too, was a settler. Here, again, were people who could take the laws of birth and death into their own hands and exercise a power greater than the laws of nature allowed. Just the night before we had talked about dabbling in the cattle business. At that moment I had some inkling of what we had inherited of desire for power and possession, of what we had lost of the ability to act from the center of life and to sense truly the balance of nature's power.

That whole first summer I felt the land circling us as the cows had done, watching us, sifting us through. The land, too, had suffered at the hands of the humans who came before us, and I sensed its hesitancy to take us to its heart. Perhaps some of the difficulty and the pain of that summer derived from our national and cultural heritage — the legacy of unpaid debt to the land that the logger and pioneer left all of us who enjoy the fruits of their conquest. I think that the land has accepted us now, and we, in our turn, have accepted the price we have to pay. We no longer have any illusions that it will be easy, if any of us ever did.

The first summer we all lived in the houses that were here when we bought the land. There were two three-room cabins and two larger, traditional houses. I lived in the big, friendly, pioneer log house — the Big House — that had been built in the 1920s, the tattered house of my first impression. With its magnificent view of the meadow and mountain peaks beyond, this house quite naturally became the center of our communal activities.

For a while I loved living right in the center of everything; I lost myself in the exhilaration of the new life and my life blended indistinguishably with that of the group. But when the first wave of change came over us and exhilaration turned chaotic around the edges, I began to feel less comfortable. Against the backdrop of the most human turmoil I had known until then, I realized I needed a personal refuge of quiet and peace, a place to be alone and renew my spirit.

At the same time, the big log house began to feel cumbersome instead of friendly; the heavy timbers, the large rectangular rooms, the multitude of shelves and cupboards started to weigh me down. As the importance of my relationship with the land became clear to me, I realized that I wanted to live closer to it. Sometime near the beginning of August I decided to make a house of my own away from the main houses, a different kind of house that would let my life grow in its own direction.

At that point in August it seemed that summer could go on forever, but I knew that the rains (which were, after all, the only reason I needed a shelter) were only a couple of months away. I had never built so much as a bookshelf, and I knew very little about the building choices that were open to me. All I really knew was that I wanted to live simply, as close and receptive to nature as possible, and I thought I'd like to try living in a round space. I needed a structure that could be put up quickly and I had only a little money to spend on materials, but as those qualifications fell naturally into the choices I made, neither was a limitation on what I wanted. I knew that Bruce had worked on construction jobs with his father; we sat down together, combined his knowledge with my intuition, and came up with an adaptation of an ancient structure, the yurt.

The yurt is a circle, a symbol of psychic wholeness, that the ancients believed exercised a specific influence on those within it. Josie, who is now eight and often spends the night with me, said it well: "I love the yurt. I feel safe and sound here. Like nothing can get me."

Yurts originated with nomadic tribes in Mongolia. Mongolian yurts are movable, made of felt and skins stretched over a latticework frame that rests on the surface of the ground. Mine is stationary; the sixteen poles that form the structure of the walls are set two feet into the ground. Sixteen more poles radiate from a central compression ring to form the roof structure. My walls are a double layer of fabric: blankets on the inside, tarps on the outside. They can be rolled up in good weather, and the air space in between the layers is good insulation when temperatures are low. The roof is four layers: burlap bags on the inside, then tarpaper, then builder's plastic, and finally burlap cement (burlap bags dipped in cement). Two skylights allow light and warmth from the sun to shine in. The floor is slate from a nearby deposit, set in cement.

The basic structural principle of the yurt is not so much that it stays up as that it can't fall down. The yurt is an interplay of forces that counteract each other to result in a stable structure. The roof poles are held rigid at the center by the compression ring. They push out on the wall poles, compounding the outward thrust they derive from their angle of placement. Thus, the roof poles' stress is all outward; it is counteracted by a cable that is wrapped around the outside top of the wall poles and equals the outward push, in effect holding it all together. That's the principle, but we weren't sure how it would really work until we tried it. The building process was punctuated by jokes about what I would be doing when the roof finally fell in.

By late August the plans were drawn. I spent September and October collecting my building materials and walking over the land to find the right site on which to build.

The land began to reveal its personality to me as I walked over its ridges, searching for a place that felt as if it were mine. The earth held me gingerly at first, not yet sure of me, as I was unsure of this new self. I had no "perfect" site in mind when I started looking; all I knew was that I wanted to be out of range of the main houses, but within reasonable walking distance. There were some practical considerations: with the last hot summer days still dawning, I knew some shade would be almost a necessity; on the other hand, I guessed it would be nice to have the warmth of the sun directly on my roof in the winter. Since I wanted to change the natural growth at my site as little as possible, its ground should be reasonably level, with no trees or large rocks.

I spent time in several different locations at different times of the day. I noticed the light, the way the shadows fell, the sounds, the smells: everything I was aware of that would be a part of my world. Early in my roamings I discovered that I liked the wide open feel of the meadow. I wandered through the forest, looking for sites, but found that I felt shut in and unsettled in the tangle of branches. I was drawn at first to sites with spectacular views and pictured the yurt perched on the brink of an awesome expanse. But nothing reached out to me, no place seemed exactly right. I continued to wander, and meanwhile got my materials organized.

I took a bow saw along on some of my walks, to cut poles for wall and roof beams. I cut live poles, live Douglas fir trees from crowded plots that needed thinning. Since I was the first to build a shelter of my own here, the source of fir saplings three inches in diameter seemed endless. I had no trouble finding clumps where the young trees grew so thick that some would be choked out by natural growth, and so I had no mental conflicts about killing a tree that might otherwise have lived. Since then, however, our city scales have fallen from our eyes, and we see three-inch saplings for the precious and fragile resource that they are. If I had known that then, I would have looked for standing trees, recently dead and not yet fallen, which had not started to decay.

I set up an area at the edge of the meadow between the two main houses to skin my poles, and spent long, pleasant hours in the slanting sun of late fall, pulling the draw knife along the length of each tree, peeling away the gray outer bark and the brown cambium layer to uncover a smooth white pole underneath. I stacked the stripped poles log cabin style, to let air circulate among them so they would dry evenly, and left them there for three weeks while I continued to search for a site. Alongside the square of poles grew a stack of other materials: empty burlap feed bags, some more than twenty years old, collected from our neighbors; a pile of slate from up the road, for my floor; rolls of tarpaper, plastic, and bags of cement, purchased from a building supply store three hours' drive south; a posthole digger, a wheel hub, and a bow saw.

My search for a place to settle the yurt went on, through September and into October, in days now sometimes streaked with rain. I found myself drawn to two or three places more strongly than to others, but still none jumped out at me and said, "Here I am. Take me."

Then one day I stopped in a place I had passed many times on my way elsewhere; it was an unassuming spot, which I had noted in passing without being interested enough to stop and inspect seriously. But that day I indulged the little voice at the back of my mind and looked at it with a practical eye. The ground was as level as I was likely to find. A big oak, the forest's sentry at the meadow's edge, stood in the southeast, offering shade on hot summer days; yet it would obligingly shed its leaves to let the sun through in winter. The site looked out onto the gentle hills of the meadow; sitting there, I felt the rush of unlimited space I realized was so important to me. Down the hill was a stream, on its way to the river, a convenient water source. There were no natural obstacles to a small structure; in fact, the natural manzanita growth suggested a circle which invited a yurt of the size I had in mind. I spent a great deal of time here, slept here, came here to read and to sit quietly. The place grew on me and into me slowly and deeply. One day I realized I had stopped looking at other sites, and I began to tell people I had found the right place.

September led into a wet fall, with heavy rains throughout October and November. I remember wondering if I would be able to do it, to really keep going and build the yurt then as I wanted to, or if I'd be forced by the weather to stop work until spring. But in late November the rains lightened up, and there were warm and relatively dry stretches throughout December and into January, when I did the actual construction. I put the last burlap bag on my roof on January 19, covered it with plastic so the cement would cure properly, and moved in that night, literally minutes before the winter rain returned with renewed seriousness.

The yurt took me nearly two months to build; that includes time out for holidays, rain, and a long bout of bronchitis. Here's the breakdown of time and expense, at 1971 prices.

*Cost of materials*

| | |
|---|---:|
| Five tarps, 8 by 10 feet, new . . . . . . . . . . . . . . . . . . | $ 50.00 |
| Cable and turnbuckle . . . . . . . . . . . . . . . . | 10.00 |
| Stove . . . . . . . . . . . . . . . . . . . . . | 10.00 |
| Stovepipe . . . . . . . . . . . . . . . . . . | 8.00 |
| Wall divider for stovepipe . . . . . . . . . . . . . . . | 2.00 |
| Screws, tacks, staples, nails . . . . . . . . . . . . . | 2.00 |
| Butyrate for skylights . . . . . . . . . . . . . . . | 10.00 |
| Creosote (preservative for poles set in ground) . . . . . . . . . | .50 |
| Rope, twine . . . . . . . . . . . . . . . . . . | 2.00 |
| Tarpaper . . . . . . . . . . . . . . . . . . . | 8.00 |
| Polyethylene plastic . . . . . . . . . . . . . . . . | 15.00 |
| Cement, 6 bags . . . . . . . . . . . . . . . . . . | 21.00 |
| | $138.50 |

*Scrounged materials:* blankets for inner walls, compression ring (wheel hub), stove cap/flashing, burlap, slate, sand for cement.

*Labor time*

| | | |
|---|---|---|
| Poles cut | 2 people | 5 hours |
| Poles stripped | 1 person | 30 hours |
| Postholes dug, poles set | 2 people | 16 hours |
| Wheel hub/compression ring prepared | 1 person | 1 hour |
| Lashing of tripod to support compression ring | 1 person | 1 hour |
| Roof poles screwed in place | 2 people | 10 hours |
| Wall poles notched, cable placed | 4 people | 1 hour |
| Construction of scaffold to lay roofing | 1 person | 2 hours |
| First three layers of roofing laid | 2 people | 7 hours |
| Skylights framed | 1 person | 3 hours |
| Burlap cement roofing laid | 5 people | 9 hours |
| Plastic protection put over new roof | 4 people | 1 hour |
| Floor laid | 4 people | 2 hours |
| Stove, stovepipe, flashing assembled | 2 people | 2 hours |

177 people-hours

This chart doesn't include any of the "hidden time" needed to collect and transport materials, gather the work force, or repair mistakes.

My mind holds many pictures of the yurt's growth. One of the clearest is of the pole frame, which was in place by the end of December. I can still close my eyes and see that circle of poles, naked white streaked with brown, rising outward into the mist.

I came out here on New Year's Eve that first year, under a full moon that cast long shadows on the frosted earth. The meadow was silver, glistening crystals of cold that crunched under my boots. The mist rose in wisps from the river and mingled with the clouds formed by my breathing. As I came over the ridge to the yurt, I was held by the skeleton of the pole frame, which stood out starkly against the gray and deep blue of the night. I walked among its shadows, reflected onto the meadow, and stopped to sit in the center of the circle. This was the first time I had been to the yurt at night since I started building. My days here had been busy ones, directed by my eagerness to move in. Now the bangs of the hammer and the rasp of the saw were gone, replaced by the silent harmony of the natural world. I realized that in the rush of activity I had missed the emergence of the yurt's personality. I felt it now: simple, modest, undemanding, a part of the hillside. Under the spell of darkness, nature reclaimed her own, and it was clear that the yurt was hers.

The building process was an act of creation. Bruce and I did most of the construction alone, learning the particular quirks of the poles and the hillside as we went. We made mistakes and miscalculations, and from time to time I felt a wave of discouragement as the date of my actual habitation slipped further away. We used no power tools; I cut the poles by hand, and we dug the postholes manually. The tone of the construction was set by the simple lines of the yurt, the quiet majesty of the site, and the growing connection between me, the yurt, and the land. It was all, most of the time, in harmony. I ingested the process as we went, until I felt myself one with the poles, the mist, the clay.

That process, that creation, laid connections very deep, or perhaps gave birth to connections already conceived. The simple grace of the yurt, which came of its own accord more than from any arrangement of mine,

still strikes me, as I sit inside and look up at the mandala formed by the roof beams and feel myself pulled up and out by the thrust of the wall poles. The yurt is as perfect an expression of who I am and who I want to be, and of the relationship between me and the land, as I can imagine.

From the yurt I look out upon meadowed and forested hills that tumble down to the river canyon and rise steeply again from the other side. The yurt rests on the shoulder of one hill and in the saddle of another. It faces east, toward the rising sun. This is my place. I feel as whole here as I ever have in my life. This is home.

# III

# Peaceful Coexistence

WHEN I WAS eight years old, a man named Sam Campbell came to speak to my third grade class. He showed movies of the skunks, raccoons, porcupines, chipmunks, and possums that populated the part of the Canadian woods where he lived with his wife in a simple log cabin. I was enraptured. Suddenly I knew beyond all doubt what I wanted to do when I grew up.

For weeks I pestered the school librarian for all of the books Sam Campbell had written, and daydreamed of a cabin of my own in some remote forest brimming with wildlife. My parents and other grown-up friends smiled at what they considered a childish fantasy, but I knew that I was absolutely serious. Nothing else in my life to that time had touched me as powerfully as that model of a simple life in the woods, surrounded by animals.

But as the months moved by, Sam Campbell and his world slipped from my daydreams and conscious memory, overtaken by the more common experiences and excitement of growing up. Yet tonight, sitting on my bed in the yurt, I am remembering that childhood dream. And I have to smile: if only my third grade teacher could see me now!

Jessica and Jojo, my constant canine companions, are sprawled over more than their rightful share of the bed. Alisha, my fat tiger-striped cat, is perched on the corner she considers hers. All three animals appear to be dozing, but I know better. At the slightest hint of something happening in the woods, which may or may not be apparent to me, Jessica and Jojo will be up and out without so much as a yawn or stretch. And Alisha's ears, even now, twitch as she interprets the messages of interest to her: the swoop of an owl, which means danger, or the rustle of a mouse in grass, which means food.

This is the fifth year I have lived in my version of a log cabin in the woods and watched summer fade from the hills. The changing of the seasons marks the passing of time, and with the rest of the natural world I feel myself shift gears. Fall means cutting wood and mending the roof. The preparations for winter are by now a familiar ritual I share with the animals that live here too. This country is still wild: bears, coyotes, and mountain lions roam the forests with raccoons, skunks, and porcupines. The bigger animals are for the most part invisible neighbors, but I know they are here, for I hear them, smell them, and see traces of their passing.

Mabel, who lives eight miles up the road and has been in these parts for over fifty years, told us in early August of last year that there wouldn't be many acorns that fall. We asked her how she knew. "Watch the bears," she said. "Aren't many around this year."

I, too, am learning to read the signs. I am conscious now of the evening chill and the morning dew, evidence of summer's end. And, now, in the hour just before sunset I sit on the hillside outside the yurt and watch the vultures fly kaleidoscopic patterns in the sky. The babies are learning to fly, rehearsing for their winter migration. They come together in pairs or larger groups until there are sometimes hundreds flying overhead, flying in figure eights and spirals, riding high on the wind. Now and then a small group breaks away to fly in counterpoint to the whole, to practice a particular formation, perhaps, and then remerges, perfectly in place.

The young ones are learning the ways of the air, I suppose: learning to fly together, to pay attention to the signals from the leaders, to ride the air currents. But in keeping with the ways of the natural world, learning is play, and from my place on the meadow, the practicing looks like a joyride. What is most striking from ground level, and what pulls at me so deeply, is the perfect harmony of the movement. The birds cannot see themselves as I see them, certainly; I have no way of knowing if they are even conscious of the patterns they are making. But what perfect, intricate, inspired patterns they are! There is a greater force at work here, clearly. The birds seem to soar to the rhythms of some celestial music, music I can feel inside as I watch. The sun sinks slowly below my horizon, and the hills across the river lose their glow. But the vultures, high in the sky, are still in the sun's path, and their wings shine golden as they reflect earthward the last rays of the day. I watch; part of me flies, too.

California's summer is hot and dry; most years there is no rain at all from June until September. This means that the hills that were green and covered with wildflowers in June turn golden brown in July, and gray around the edges in late August. By September, the earth needs rain. This year it is early October, and the summer drought has not yet broken. The meadow is barren, its soil cracked and parched, its life withdrawn. The whole world thirsts. The grass has long since disappeared; all that is left on the meadow's face are lonely skeletons of grass and camphor weed. The animals that graze on the meadow grasses are hungry.

We have kept our herd of Hereford cattle at thirty by selling one steer for every newborn calf each season. Three dairy cows — Bonnie, Bebe, and Germany — and thirteen horses mingle with the Herefords, and all of them look to the meadow for their breakfast, lunch, and dinner. This is a heavy load for the meadow to feed, and the burden has never been more evident than it is now, with fall already upon us, and still no rain.

The cows have turned to eating oak leaves in the absence of grass. But the horses would keep on pulling away at the memory of grass on the meadow, delving ever deeper into its soil, and jeopardizing ever more its fragile ecosystem, if we would let them. Instead, we have decided to keep the horses in corrals until the rain brings new feed, asking them to exchange their freedom for a daily bale of hay. I'm not sure they think it's a good bargain as they run back and forth inside the pole fences, gazing out onto the hills they love to run upon, tails flying in their wake. But it's the least we can do for the meadow.

Last night I ate dinner at the Big House, which still serves as the focus for our communal activities. Jessica was unusually anxious to leave, telling me that it was time to go at least a half hour before I made any move on my own. Jojo was waiting for us on the porch. We started the half-mile walk home through the meadow, pungent with October odors. The dogs left me at the crest of the first hill and raced through the night toward the yurt, as is their custom. But last night, instead of waiting for me there, Jessica ran back to meet me as I rounded the second hill, prancing in her eagerness to tell me to hurry. I could hear Jojo barking in the background, from the vicinity of the yurt. I stepped up my pace; Jessica, impatient, ran relays between me and the yurt.

There was no moon, and the night was very black despite the stars. I couldn't see anything. But as I approached the yurt I realized that the dogs were right: something *was* amiss. The sound of heavy breathing came from inside, and I could hear the crunch of large teeth chewing. In the still night air it sounded like an elephant at the very least.

A bear? A wild pig? I went through the list of creatures I knew inhabited the woods around, some of whom I didn't fancy meeting in my house on a black night such as this, even with two dogs eager to help.

Taking a deep breath, I struck a match to light the night enough to get a look at what was making all the noise. In the brief flash of light from the flame I saw not a bear, not a wild boar, but cows. *Two* cows. Bebe, the black calf we had raised to a healthy size, was resting on my bed, apparently waiting her turn to get at the dog food which Bonnie, her horns lowered, was enthusiastically munching, grinding, and swallowing.

I didn't know whether to yell or cry or laugh. Jojo was running around the yurt barking, furious at the impudence of the cows not only to help themselves to her food but also to ignore her increasingly vehement protests.

I struck another match and lit the kerosene lamp closest to the door. The light forced the cows to acknowledge the fact that I was there, and with a perception I don't usually attribute to cows, they seemed to realize that I wasn't pleased to find them in my house. Bebe, in fact, looked downright chagrinned. She gave me a long, sorrowful look that seemed to say: "I'm sorry I came. Please get me out of here."

Indeed: get them out. I realized that wasn't going to be an easy task. How exactly did they get *in*, anyway?

I had never before appreciated just how big cows are. They suddenly seemed monstrous compared to the proportions of the yurt. Their bulk filled the few square feet of floor space, leaving very little room to maneuver. And the dogs weren't making the situation any easier. Jojo, taking

[ 39 ]

courage from my obvious displeasure, was now darting in to nip at Bonnie's heels between her noisy circles of the yurt.

"Well, girls," I thought, "you got in here somehow; let's see if you can get out with a little help from me." I decided to try Bebe first. I went over to her, turned her head in the direction of out, and gave her a push. A little decisive action appeared to break her spell. She turned almost delicately, lowered her head so as not to hit the ceiling, gracefully managed to avoid breaking the kerosene lamp just inches from her right flank, and made her exit.

Bonnie must have guessed that her meal was nearly over when Bebe deserted her, but she held on to her apparent control of the situation. She raised her head slowly, looked straight at me with undisguised disdain, and licked her lips as if to say, "That was a good dinner, but I'm full just now, so I'll be on my way." She rolled out the door just as Jojo closed in for the final attack. Once outside, both cows allowed themselves to be chased over the hill by the barking dogs, who returned looking very satisfied with their defense of the yurt.

I noted in disbelief that nothing had been broken, nothing even knocked from the shelves, and my bed appeared none the worse for a cow's having sat on it. The only real evidence of the dinner party was the heavy bovine scent that lingered in the air.

It was hard to begrudge the cows a little nourishment more substantial and handy than oak leaves, considering the circumstances of the season. I poured myself a cup of water and went to sit outside under the oak tree. Quiet had returned to the meadow, broken only by the now familiar sounds of the night. I sat for a long time, listening. Before I finally rose to go to sleep, I joined the rest of the natural world in a heartfelt prayer for the turning of the season. Rain, please, rain, soon, rain.

Wet or dry, there are bugs. And despite my enduring love for the natural world, these little creatures have always given me the creeps. It never occurred to me, in my days of dreaming about living in the woods like Sam Campbell, that there might be *bugs* in his cabin.

Years of summer camp brought me into close contact with all kinds of insects, but did little to dim my fear. When I was very young, I called my father to kill them for me. Later I learned that if I wanted them dead I would have to do it myself, which was almost as bad as living with them.

When I was a child we lived in a house that stood in the midst of a grove of tall oak trees. The oaks made a wonderful home for an army of woodroaches, one or two of whom would occasionally find their way into my bedroom. The roaches were up to an inch in length, with long, curving antennae and wings that folded into a tough shell on their back. They were completely harmless; I was terrified of them.

Each night, before I dared to enter my bedroom, I flicked on the light from the hallway and searched every square inch of wall space, remembering especially to crane my neck to see the ceiling. On the infrequent but always anticipated occasions when I actually found a woodroach, my dilemma increased: now what? The thought of killing it made me nauseous, but there seemed no alternative. Sleeping with the roach in the room was out of the question, and picking it up to move it elsewhere never occurred to me.

So I would sit in front of the bug for many long minutes, heart beating fast, trying to get up the courage to hit it. I would decide again on the best weapon to absorb some of the horrible crunch of crushing the exoskeleton. Finally I would reach for a book, eyes glued on the roach, and talk to myself. "Now," I'd say, "now!" And finally I would do it — smash the bug with all my might. One hard hit, and it was dead, smeared on my silver-patterned wallpaper.

That little melodrama is not an exaggeration. Yet, strangely, the wild things that I now know best are just the ones that used to evoke such fear. The yurt is populated by successive legions of earwigs, stink bugs, wasps, grasshoppers, daddy longlegs, and caterpillars, as well as numerous individual beetles, spiders, and moths. This house is as much theirs as mine, and I find that I dislike being the biggest occupant. I try to interrupt their natural existence as little as possible, and for the most part we coexist quite peaceably. In exchange for not disturbing them, I am rewarded with a chance to view their mating, egg hatching, and metamorphosing.

I can't explain my own metamorphosis from bug fearer to admirer except to suspect that like all prejudices, mine yielded to a glimmer of knowledge. Sedg, a friend and visitor who has a college degree's worth of spider lore in his head, has helped. He comes to the ranch armed with identification books, a light that attaches to his head for night hunting, a sheet onto which he shakes spiders from an overhanging bush, and a suitcase full of vials for the unusual specimens he expects to find. His enthusiasm is contagious, and now that I can call the spiders by name, I no longer jump when I see a ball with eight legs walk across my pillow. Instead I think, "Oh, a black and yellow argiope; I wonder where she'll spin her web?"

That interest in spiders seems to have diffused my apprehension of most insects, as well as worms, lizards, and their relatives. Last winter I became quite fond of a banana slug that appeared one fall day and stayed through the cold months until late spring. He (or she) was about four inches long, yellowish-green, and one day allowed me to turn him over so

[ 42 ]

I could inspect his strange translucent belly. He spent the winter sliding ever so slowly around the walls of the yurt, leaving a trail of slime. I grew used to watching out for his whereabouts so I would not step on him by mistake during one of his ventures to the floor, and I found that I missed him when he disappeared in the spring.

But not all of the creatures with whom I share these hills are harmless. In addition to the bears, mountain lions, bobcats, and wild pigs, which could inflict sizable injury if provoked, there are scorpions, black widow spiders, and rattlesnakes.

One hot evening in our second summer while my brother Bob was visiting from Michigan, the two of us were walking home to the yurt from the Big House. There was no moon, but the stars were bright, and we carried no flashlight. I had discovered long before that the bright beam of a flashlight in effect obliterates everything beyond its limited reach. I preferred to rely on my developing night vision, and starlight was easily bright enough to find my way home on a summer night.

At the time, I held several misconceptions about rattlesnakes. I had pieced together enough fragments of information to believe that (1) the rattlesnakes here didn't possess venom strong enough to kill a person; (2) they weren't aggressive and would always move away rather than attack if there was a choice; and (3) they weren't out at night. A short time later Andy punctured myths 1 and 2 with a couple of old-timer stories; by then he didn't need to tell me number 3 was wishful thinking.

Bob and I were so engrossed in talking that we missed the path to the back of the yurt that I usually take, and so we circled around to the front instead. Just as we were almost at the door, I heard a sound I had never heard before but that I recognized the moment I heard it: the buzz of a rattlesnake. It was coming from the path behind the yurt, where the dogs had just been.

I rushed into the yurt to grab a flashlight, found to my relief that the dogs were safely inside, and then pushed the beam in the direction of the continuing sound. Sure enough, there was a rattlesnake, a big one, coiled, tail vibrating furiously — and there was my cat Alisha within a foot of the menacing arrow-shaped head. The next second, to my horror, she reared up on her hind feet and gave the snake a resounding swat with her right front paw.

I felt my stomach lurch. Weak with fear, I moved closer, calling Alisha, "Here, kitty, kitty, kitty. Alisha, come here. Come on, kitty."

The snake continued to rattle angrily, its tongue darting in and out. But for some reason it did not strike. Alisha, perhaps feeling she had made her point, and clearly aware of the potential for harm from the creature whose face she had just slapped, inched backward slowly, step by step, never once taking her eyes off that triangular head. Finally she was far enough out of range for me to grab her. She remained tense and alert in my arms, heart pounding under my hand.

This was the first rattlesnake I had seen on the land, but not the first the group had encountered. Of the four snakes seen around the houses the first summer, three were killed and the fourth slid away. This second summer we had discussed capturing and relocating the snakes as an alternative to killing them. We all agreed we didn't want to kill snakes we came across in the woods, but many of us didn't care to share living areas with a creature that could effect such unpleasant surprises. I hadn't really decided how I felt about the question, but now, holding onto a cat who wanted very much to get down and keep track of that snake, watching the snake continue to rattle and test the air with its tongue, I realized I'd sleep easier that night if it was elsewhere. I asked Bob to go get Bruce to help.

While Bob was gone, I kept my flashlight on the snake so I wouldn't lose him. He was about four feet long, and fat. I speculated that he had recently eaten, which may have made him less eager to strike at Alisha. Slowly he uncoiled, stopped rattling, and lay almost perfectly camouflaged among the rocks and grass. I examined his markings, not diamond but pentagonal, and his head and eight rattles. There was no question of his being a gopher snake, which has similar markings but neither rattles nor has arrow-shaped head. As the rattler began to move, I was struck by the dignity of his movement. I knew he could move fast if he chose, but now his pace was slow and almost majestic, as was fitting for this most respected of snakes.

I wished Bob and Bruce would hurry. The snake was angling toward the yurt, a spot I didn't want him to decide he liked. I called the dogs, who came straight to my side and safety and seemed strangely unaware of all the unusual activity. They, who are supersensitive to most signs of life in the woods, seemed not to notice this four-foot reptile that was about to invade their house. Alisha, by contrast, still squirmed in my arms, obviously wanting to get down where she could follow the action. But I held tight and watched the snake crawl in and out of the tarps near my bed at the back of the yurt. I supposed he was only seeking shelter, but the thought of his finding it there made me very nervous.

Finally I heard voices, and Bob and Bruce came running. Bruce had forked stick and a burlap bag: a snake relocation kit. I was very glad to see him.

"Nice night, isn't it?" he greeted me with a smile. And then to the snake, "Snattlerake, snattlerake, it's time for a new home."

[ 45 ]

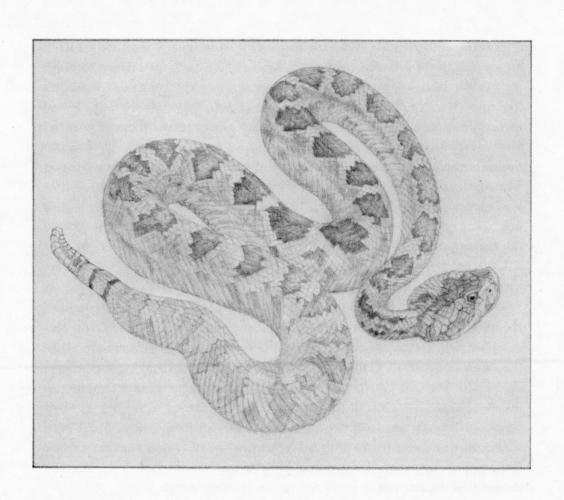

As I watched, still fighting to keep Alisha out of the way and receiving an armful of scratches for my trouble, they coaxed the snake away from the yurt and out into the open. The snake seemed so reluctant to fight, refusing even to go to the trouble of coiling again, that Bruce decided to escort him a safe distance down the meadow rather than force him into the bag. More than anything, he seemed to want a nice quiet place to curl up and digest his meal away from all those poking sticks. By this time, fortified by the presence of two other human beings, I found that my nerves had quieted to the point that I felt some compassion for the snake's obvious desire to get away. From that perspective, down the meadow seemed far enough, so I agreed.

I stayed at the yurt, glad for a chance to release the angry feline in my arms. Bob and Bruce returned in forty-five minutes and reported that the snake had gone peaceably half a mile down the hillside and crawled under a big boulder. They assured me everything was fine.

And, indeed, everything was. After my initial panic when I saw Alisha slap the snake's head, I realized I was glad finally to see the creature that is the object of so much fear and folklore. I found that he seemed to be an animal after all. An animal with appetites, needs, and a particular talent for self-defense. Having seen this snake face to face, I could no longer harbor fantasies of rattlers lurking in the woods, waiting to inflict lethal harm on unsuspecting humans. Still, I had no illusions about a rattlesnake's good intentions and was very glad not to have him underfoot.

That, however, proved to be something of a false hope. I didn't see that snake or any other again that summer, but each summer since then a large rattlesnake has appeared once at the yurt. Whether it is the same snake or another one, I don't know. But "down the meadow," as I since have learned, wasn't much of a relocation, since rattlesnakes commonly range much farther than that in search of food. Alisha usually discovers the visitor first, but she has been more cautious since that first encounter. This summer she merely got close enough to provoke a rattle and then made a hasty but careful retreat. So did the snake.

I am still nervous at the thought of sharing living quarters with a rattlesnake, but it hasn't yet come to that point, and I expect Alisha will let me know if it does.

And I now carry a flashlight on hot summer nights.

# IV
# Simplifying

FROM MY bed I can hear the sound of the crows calling out as they fly zigzags into the morning sun. I turn over, stretch, and breathe deeply of the fresh morning air. The air is crisp, these late fall days, and I must move quickly to lay a fire before losing the warmth I carry from the bed. Once the match is struck, the yurt heats in minutes as flames spread from kindling to the bigger logs in the stove. I pour water into a pan to heat for washing and put the teapot on the back of the stove. When the wash water is warm, I pour it into the basin and bathe. I put a couple of big logs on the fire, spread my quilt on the levelest part of the floor, and start my day in silence, with a few simple yoga exercises and a forty-five-minute meditation.

When I finish, the tea water is nearly boiling. I choose a tea from the shelves or break a few leaves from the bunches hanging from the roof beams, and toast a piece of bread over an open burner on the stove as the tea steeps. Then the tea is ready, I pour myself a cup, butter the toast, and sit down to enjoy my breakfast and the wandering of my thoughts.

My morning ritual ends here. From this point each day takes on a character of its own depending on the season, the work that needs doing, and my choice. The freedom to choose the demands on my own time is an important one for me, and a great part of what my move to the yurt has come to symbolize.

Our earliest group efforts were directed toward achieving a measure of self-sufficiency and independence from the outside world. After two years of hard and nearly full-time work, we had an acre-and-a-half garden, two dairy cows, a two-acre orchard, seven acres of alfalfa, twenty chickens, five horses, and thirty Herefords. Establishing and maintaining all that activity meant building a new dam and laying irrigation pipe; fencing the hayfield, orchard, and garden; building a milking shed, corrals, and a barn; and keeping the truck, tractor, and cars in good repair. The work was good and necessary, and working together was important to our overriding goal of learning to live harmoniously with each other and with the land. But as the second year drew to a close and the basis for a working homestead was pretty well established, and still there were more plans for more projects the next spring, I realized that all the activity was obscuring my real reasons for moving to the country.

I caught myself thinking, "Well, when the garden is planted, then I can relax and enjoy the summer evenings." Or, "maybe after the orchard fence is in place, I'll have a few days to camp down by the river." But I finally realized that such "when it's done" thinking was an illusion. There was *always* something more to do. And although others seemed to find meaning and fulfillment in the continued development of the ranch, I found that the sheer force of the activity was keeping me locked in patterns of busyness I had known before I moved to the land and was crowding out the newer and quieter work of getting to know myself, which was more important to me.

When I realized that the work wasn't going to wind down of its own accord, I saw that the only way to stop was to stop. And when I finally did that, I realized that most of the things that we were working so hard to provide, I would just as soon do without. That meant that I would rather drink fir needle tea than milk a cow every day, rather do without eggs than build a chicken house and care for chickens.

I, who had always been busy and had always had more food, clothing, and shelter than I needed, wanted to find out what I really did need and want. I wanted to question my ideas of comfort and convenience, to stop the psychic noise of constant activity to find what was at the core. I wanted time and space enough to allow the internal changes I could feel taking shape inside me.

And so I gradually detached myself from daily activity which revolved around the Big House. Instead I began eating more of my meals at the yurt and spending more of my time there. Within — and sometimes pushing — the limits of being a member of a family that had decided to have chickens, dairy cows, and a large garden, I tried to let my life run free enough of those demands that I could find my own way. The continuing effort to find the proper balance between my own needs and my communal responsibilities has cultivated patience, understanding, and good manners on all sides — and has incidentally saved me from becoming a fanatic, primitive style.

The yurt is furnished simply. To the left of the entry are floor-to-ceiling shelves, which hold food in animal-proof containers, and a fold-out table. Then there is a desk, a working table, two sections of bookshelves, and another set of shelves for my clothes. The two beds are covered with spreads that shed dog hair and paw prints easily. A raincoat, a few heavy shirts, a towel, bunches of herbs, a frying pan, and three small pots hang from nails pounded into the roof beams. Two gallon water jugs, a kerosene jar, and the wood bin lie around the yurt's circumference. And scattered around the table and desk and between the shelves are two chairs, a stool, and a cushion.

Simple, colorful, cozy. There is very little at hand that I do not use, so my daily life is not cluttered with things I must maintain but which render no service. The furnishings are scaled down to the nearly essential. But austerity is not the tone; rather, the yurt feels extraordinarily comfortable and warm. Severity is not the tone of my life here; rather, simplicity — and the freedom that accompanies it.

My body was overweight and out of tune when it arrived here. I exulted in the hard physical labor of the first summer, feeling muscles long unused become tight and strong. My body slowly began to do what I asked of it, and to feel good. I ate well — whole grains, home-grown vegetables, local fruit — but often too much. I find now that my body feels lightest, most responsive, and has the most energy, when I eat sparingly. For the first time in my life, I feel trim, lean, tight. Exercise is a pleasure, a tuning, rather than an uncomfortable exertion.

So I am glad that wood needs to be split daily for the winter fire. The maul is heavy, and I can package all my restlessness behind the force needed to swing it up and down onto the logs. It feels good to breathe deeply with the exertion, to inhale the cool, moist air, and to feel the sharp crack of the wood as it splits. I stack the split wood under the eaves of the yurt and bring in enough to fill my wood box.

I can clean the yurt adequately in fifteen minutes and thoroughly in forty-five. I dust the shelves, take food scraps to the compost pile, shake the rugs, sweep the floor, fill the lamps.

The simple tasks of a simple existence. Performing them brings me in direct contact with the material plane of life, and yet somehow releases my spirit. There is a transcendence hidden in simplicity. I noticed it first while lashing together bay laurel shoots for my bed. It was the first fall, and the smell of rain was barely in the air. I had cut the young branches myself, with a corn chopper, to the size of the width of the bed, and carried them to a place on the hillside in front of where the yurt was to be. I sat on the ground and lashed shoot to shoot with binder's twine, winding the twine around and back and through, pulling it tight, adding another shoot, repeating the process. It was simple work, but time-consuming: I spent three long afternoons before I was finished.

But the time didn't matter; in fact, I was almost sorry when the last shoot was lashed and the bed was ready to be attached to the bigger logs that made its frame. I had been very happy in the rhythm of the work. Sitting on the hill under the sun, working with simple materials of nature, I felt a merging of self, spirit, and matter. The work became an exercise, the repetition an act of centering — a tool to quiet my mind, to soothe my restlessness, to liberate my spirit.

It doesn't work that way, of course, unless you have the time. If splitting wood is only one of a long list of chores for the day, it's hard to enjoy the rhythm of the maul's swing — and central heating is suddenly very appealing.

But what I found, as I simplified my life to a scale that was inspired by the yurt, was that my world slowed down and there weren't so many things to do. Individual tasks take longer, but since there aren't as many of them, I perform them with genuine pleasure. And even more important, splitting wood to keep myself warm and carrying water to quench my thirst provide a contact with the basic elements of my survival that satisfies some deep craving in my spirit. I suspect this is the same craving that, if deprived of its natural fulfillment, looks for relief instead in a new dress, a bigger car, a second home — in "more."

I began to see some of the hidden costs of such conveniences as electricity and repairmen. True comfort now seems to me to mean a life whose physical dimensions are within my grasp. The sense of purpose and fulfillment that comes from direct participation in my own survival is a luxury beyond the reach of money, and one I wouldn't trade for all the vacuum cleaners, telephones, and electric mixers that money — and a location closer to town — might provide.

That is not to say that I don't recognize the benefits of some of civilization's offerings. Chain saws and automobiles are important parts of my life. But I am very aware of the intrusion into my feeling of wholeness of such machines that I don't yet know how to repair or maintain myself. That is reason enough for me to try to limit my world to conveniences that do not meet that qualification.

Is mine a life of deprivation? No, not in the least. This life is supremely enough; I don't want more. Richness and leisure and liberation of spirit are the rewards of simplicity, and satisfaction and fulfillment from physical involvement with life preempt a spiraling desire for more.

When I first moved to the yurt, I had no money to tempt me to accumulate things or conveniences beyond the bare essentials. I was in good health, without a family to care for, and blessed with seasonal freedom from ranch work. That situation allowed me to try a simple lifestyle with an ease I might not have otherwise had. And now I find that even though I have some pocket money these days and have gone through periods of ill health, my ideas of comfort and convenience have been permanently altered.

For four years I carried my water from the stream rather than lay the pipes that would bring water to my door. Carrying water was part of my weekly rhythm, walking to the stream kept me in touch with the plants that grew alongside it, and carrying two heavy gallons of water uphill made me very conscious of my use of it. I learned to wash greasy pans right away while they were easiest to clean with the least amount of water, and I asked each gallon of water to serve as many purposes as I could devise. Water used to boil an egg became dishwater (without soap), and finally ended up in the dogs' bowl.

Last summer the fire hazard was particularly high, and we decided that the yurt needed a supply of ready water as a safety measure. With reluctance, I agreed. But I feared the laying of the black pipe might be the first step on a road away from survival-level simplicity, and I shrank from the changes it might begin in my life.

I need not have worried. Because carrying water had never felt like a hardship, the availability of running water didn't start a chain reaction of modernization in the yurt. If I had any illusions about the time saved by conveniences, the hours that I spend repairing the black pipe remind me of the true cost of water at the turn of a faucet. But most important, I am still careful of the amount of water I use. That is what means the most to me — not the fact of carrying water or splitting wood, but the sense of water and trees as a precious gift, and the determination to be a careful, responsible member of the earth that provides them.

It is late November, and the twenty-fourth day in a row that it has rained at least part of the day. Streams run like roadmaps on the face of the meadow, and the summer drought seems months behind us. Last night and today the wind has been a furious accomplice to the rain. I sense its coming from far away, hear it charging up the hill, feel its palm open to give the yurt a resounding thwomp. The tarps bellow, the door blankets fly in, the lamp threatens to go out, the roof beams shudder. I tuck in the blankets around the obvious gaps, lay logs along the bottom edge of the door, and brace myself for the next gust, which I can already hear coming like a steam engine from away up the river.

The rain pounds on my roof; its noise drowns out the crackle of my fire and hides the sound of my tea water boiling. There are voices hidden in the rain and in the wind, too many voices sometimes. My nerves are battered by the unending artillery of sound. The wind frightens me in the force of its rage, and the rain, sometimes so soothing, today seems relentless and driving.

My face is tight from days of wood smoke, my body stiff from inactivity. I know from experience that a storm always seems worse from inside than it feels when I am outside in the middle of it. Still, the thought of soothing my nerves and my muscles by taking a walk makes me shudder. It is strangely hard to break out of this cocoon the yurt has become. Even a dwelling as simple as this has closed me off; my mind and the force of inertia have let it become the fortress my comfort-oriented self thought it needed.

Finally the storm breaks for a moment, and I force myself to pull on boots and a raincoat and step outside. As I should have known, the mist in the air eases the tension in my face immediately, and I take in a deep breath of the rich brown smell of the earth. The sky is a collage of shape and color, herded by the wind into gray, brown, and black patterns. I can feel my eyes relax with the broadening of my horizons, and drink deeply of the expanse of land and sky around me.

Intermission over, the lights dim once again, and the storm ushers rain back onto its stage. Some of it drips onto my nose from the hood of my raincoat. Then the wind returns and drives the rain into my face, up my sleeves, down the back of my neck. I crouch under a tree, and watch the Douglas firs on the hill across the stream bend with the wind. The gusts of cold air push against me, too, and take my breath away. My heart beats faster, but from excitement now. Here, within the storm, I feel its fury still, but I am no longer afraid.

The rain elevates the simple facts of warmth and dryness to a level of conscious pleasure. Dry firewood, a good raincoat, and a pair of boots that are both watertight and comfortable are real joys. It took me three years to find the proper footwear for this climate. I finally settled on a combination rubber and leather boot, and am at last experiencing the luxury of dry feet.

But there is another side to those simple comforts, a side that was important for me to learn: it's not so bad to be cold or wet. In fact, being here has led me to rediscover what every child knows intuitively — getting wet can sometimes be sheer delight. I remember playing in a summer rainstorm on the shore of Lake Michigan when I was six years old. In my bathing suit, I sang and danced and giggled on a landing overlooking the lake, overflowing with glee as rainwater ran through my hair, into my eyes and mouth, and down my back. Somewhere in the process of growing up, I lost the memory of that glee and replaced it with the conviction that getting wet was uncomfortable. But here I am finding that my ideas of comfort are just more habits, part of the baggage that has weighed down my life and which I am now calling into question.

I think of the Indians who lived in these hills before me: how they lived in harmony and intimacy with the great, the mysterious, and the mundane forces of nature. And then I think of myself and how I am still not able to quiet that little voice inside that insists on loading me up with equipment and supplies for a trip into the wilderness, or even for a few days at the river. I have begun to learn the extent of my capacities here, but only barely begun. The ghosts of the Indian children who lived here must laugh at the hesitation I still have about spending a night in the rain, or the effort I still exert in creating my idea of comfort.

That's it, of course: my *idea* of comfort. What the yurt has offered me, above all, is the chance to challenge my ideas and to shake off or replace those that seem to restrict rather than liberate my spirit. That work continues. I have found it is not so easy as moving to the country, or living primitively, to calm the restless storms of thoughts and desires that swirl about from time to time in my head. I still feel harried, overburdened, and afraid sometimes. But there is a difference. I can no longer blame my job, or my schedule, or my friends for my problems. The yurt and its simple ways have freed me from the pressure of externally imposed demands so that I can see the real source of pressure — my own poor, tired, still-too-cluttered head. I see now quite clearly what was always true: I am the creator of my universe, responsible for the nature and functioning of my world.

But what do I *do* here?

Some days I stretch breakfast into late afternoon, curled near the fire with a book. Other days I write, or walk to the river, or chop wood, or answer letters. I bake eight loaves of bread at the Big House nearly once a week, and less frequently I spend a long afternoon baking a huge batch of granola. Three times a week I work with Kristine and Josie on reading and writing. Some days there are things to do together: beans to shell, projects to plan, a kitchen to paint. Other seasons bring hay hauling, summer camps, and wilderness trips.

But I spend most of my time alone. There is a hermit strong within me, and I find energy and strength in solitude. Long, golden, uncharted hours of contemplation, of wandering among the hills and trees I know so well, of sitting silently upon a crag overlooking the river canyon: these are the vital hours. The rest were born to support these, and were born from these.

The warmth I find in the rolling lines of the meadow, the breath of life that comes to me from the first spring wildflower: for and from these moments comes energy to split wood and bake bread. I split wood for a fire to keep me warm and in good health so I can sit at the edge of the river tomorrow, and yet I sit at the edge of the river so I can bake bread that afternoon. There is a merging into evenness, a moment when sweeping the floor slides into meditation, so that each moment is as precious as the next, and each carries within it the secret that was whispered to me first on the vultures' wings.

The hermit in me dominates, but I am not the hermit. In solitude I have found deep connections with others: I feel family, friends, and strangers come together in my dreams. The hermit is my center, the source from which my energy rises, but the sunrise and the owl's call and the touch of other humans give it nourishment.

I spend most of my time alone, but I am always startled when someone asks if I'm lonely. Lonely? There are moments, yes, but they do not set the tone. This is a life of such plenty that it overflows. From inside the yurt, I can feel twilight stretching over the meadow. I fold up the type-writer for the day, and turn from my desk to see the dogs and cat curled up together on the bed. From across the river I can hear a coyote howl. I light the lamp, put on a pot of rice for dinner, and stoke up the fire. The muscles in my back and neck are stiff from hours of typing; I can feel them relax into the pulls of my favorite yoga positions. The rain has finally lightened. I spread my quilt for the second time today and listen to the gentle falling of the rain as daylight fades from the sky and I enter my evening meditation.

# V

# Economic Survival

I ARRIVED on the land with $1000 in personal savings and an idea that money had no place in my vision of the way the world ought to be. I had found that money too often was an artificial barrier between people and that it promoted a false scale of the value of time and effort and need. In my heart I wanted to do away with money, live generously to the extent of my abilities, and be provided for generously because it was my right of birth.

That vision now seems not only hopelessly naive but also a little irresponsible. I have learned that money is just one of the apparent inequalities that life has handed us for our entertainment and enrichment, with which we must deal forthrightly. But some of the underlying feeling of that vision, a determination not to let money — the need or want of it — rule my life, is with me still and has proven good company on the difficult road to economic survival here.

We are a group with the same extremes of wealth that exist in the rest of the world. Some of us have no money at all and others have enough to live comfortably for a lifetime. There was never any question that we were all in this together, that the ranch was our long-term home, and that we would struggle through the economic realities together without letting them deter us from our larger purposes. Our only difficulties have come from trying to translate those unquestionables into day-to-day and month-to-month working realities: who would pay what and when and how. We have tried very hard to let the financial structure reflect other, deeper truths in our lives; for that reason, as those truths or our perceptions of them have changed, so have our finances. It has nevertheless been hard. The reasons are several, including the time and energy demands of a venture such as this, the dearth of skills among us that are marketable from the country, and the urban-centered U.S. economy.

In the beginning, it seemed very natural to let those who had inherited family money pay the down payment and the first two mortgage payments in order to give us time to get on our communal feet. After the second year we hoped to be financially self-sufficient and to generate money for mortgage and operating expenses with group projects. That time projection proved to be a bit optimistic, but it set up an initial framework for us to plan within. There has never been any question about who owned the land — we all own it. Those who contributed to the first payments have their names on the title now, but when our pending nonprofit status is awarded, they will legally donate the land to the nonprofit corporation.

We all put the money we brought with us into the operating expenses of the land. Those of us without a renewable source of income ran through our personal savings (my $1000 was a typical sum) in the first year. Those who could afford to — which mostly meant those who had a steady income from invested inherited capital — continued to contribute to monthly expenses past the two-year mark when we realized that it was going to take us longer than that to get on our feet, but half the monthly budget and most

[ 62 ]

of the mortgage payment after the second year did come from group projects, as planned.

The first of those projects came in the spring of our first year. By then we were feeling settled enough on the land to begin casting about for a way to bring in some income. When we met an organic farmer who held the harvest rights to an old, unpruned apricot orchard that was about to be razed for a housing development, it seemed like just what we were looking for. The farmer belonged to a group that owned another orchard, which demanded all their time, and they were willing to sell us the fruit from the old orchard at a good price if we would pick it ourselves. We planned to bring the picked "cots" back to the ranch to dry for sale. The knowledge that the orchard would be bulldozed a month after cot season and that this last fruit would go unused if we did not pick it added a measure of mission to our plans.

Apricot country is a long day's drive from the ranch, south toward San Francisco and then east through wine country to that part of the Sacramento Valley that grows a great proportion of the nation's fruit. The weather turned hot the morning we left the ranch, and by four hours down the road it was sizzling. Kathy and I drove the ranch's '49 International truck, and even the breeze from the open windows couldn't keep my blouse dry of perspiration.

When we turned east off Highway 101, the scenery began to change and I realized I was entering a world far removed in kind and spirit from the ranch. We drove on a winding two-lane road, over and around lovely small hills dotted with grapes and fruit trees. Here and there a winery nestled into a hillside. The gentleness of the scenery was belied by the force of the heat, which seemed to be increasing even though it was late after-noon. As the hills smoothed out into longer and longer fertile valleys, I saw migrant workers bent over in the sun-drenched fields. "How can they work in this heat?" I wondered.

Finally we reached apricot country, and the fields were filled with trees dripping with ripening orange-yellow fruit. We turned onto the main street in Summers and stopped to wait for the rest of the ranchers. Summers is a grand old town from another era: wide, tree-lined streets, stately frame buildings set well back from the sidewalks. I half expected a stagecoach to appear around the corner. But there was no stagecoach — or much of anything else. Although this was the peak of the commercial season, the streets were strangely quiet. From time to time a huge truck filled with crates of apricots destined for a distant market passed through, but other than that, ours was one of the few vehicles in sight. The four or five people we saw didn't seem to be talking or smiling. "Perhaps it's the heat," I thought, "or the long day's drive, but something feels strange here. There is a charge to the air that almost seems like tension." But tension seemed out of place on the lovely old streets, and the arrival of two other truckloads of ranchers quickly pushed away the thought. I was to remember it not too many hours later.

Our friends the organic farmers had told us we could sleep in an apricot orchard near their place. After a spicy dinner in a tiny Mexican restaurant, we followed their directions, or so we thought, and stretched out our sleeping bags at the edge of a field of trees laden with fruit still green, but ripe enough to fill the air with the aroma of apricots. We climbed into our sleeping bags early, thinking of the long day ahead. One by one, we made peace with the continued but finally waning heat and an army of attacking mosquitoes, and fell wearily asleep just as the stars were settling in overhead.

Some hours later, I was startled awake by a shout and opened my eyes to a searchlight shining full in my face. As I tried to remember who I was and what I was doing lying there in that dusty field, I realized that the voice behind the searchlight was asking the same questions. Or rather he was shouting the same questions in a tone that indicated he didn't care much about the answers. Ranger tried to answer anyway, his voice slow from sleep. At about the same time we all realized that there was a rifle in the hand that held that awful light and the rifle was pointed at us. Our minds working suddenly more quickly, we also realized that it didn't really matter what answers we had to the questions, or that it was the middle of the night, or that we had driven a long way and had a long day ahead rescuing the last fruit from a doomed orchard. Nothing mattered but the fact that we were in someone else's orchard and we might steal his apricots. And the someone had a gun pointed at us and was quite serious about using it if we didn't move. Immediately.

With remarkable speed, all of us gathered our scattered belongings, stuffed them inside our sleeping bags, put on shoes, and went. Too tired to do much more than fit the missing piece in the puzzle of why the air had seemed so strange to me in town, I stumbled with the others across the road into a ditch that the man with the gun had okayed as sleeping territory, climbed into my bag once again, and tried to pick up my dreams.

I woke the next morning with a more sophisticated understanding of where we were and the serious business that was under way. As we drove to the orchard we were to pick, I noticed that barbed wire, electrified fences, and men with guns surrounded every field. I hoped there would be no more mistakes on our part.

We found our orchard without trouble and met our organic farming friends, who had agreed to give us a quick lesson in picking cots. They warned us that these trees would be harder to pick than the commercial orchards because they hadn't been pruned in years. Since that also meant that the owner hadn't bothered to spray the fruit, we were glad to contend with the extra difficulty. Our friends gave us a truckload of empty crates (called lugs), pointed out the water faucet, promised they would return at dark to see how we had done, and left us to go to their own orchard.

Though the sun was just barely over the horizon, the heat of the day was already rising fast. I tied a sweatband around my head, picked up an empty crate, and got to work. The trees were old, their bark wrinkled and their branches tangled, but the fruit was delicious. Soon I settled into a rhythm, learned to pick with both hands, to place rather than drop the fruit in the crate, and to reject the cots that were so ripe they would rot before the return trip. I watched with satisfaction as my lug filled.

When the branches I could reach from the ground were all picked and I climbed into the tree and balanced my lug on a convenient fork, I began to understand why our friends had warned us that the trees were unpruned. Branches were everywhere, sticking me in the back, in the eye, barring the way to the best fruit, right where I needed to put my foot next. In trees that have been pruned, care has been taken to remove enough branches so that the fruit is easy to get to and therefore can be picked efficiently. My second lug filled much more slowly.

The hours passed, the heat rose steadily, tree followed tree. In the early morning I had chattered excitedly to those working near me and watched lug after lug move from the empty pile to be filled with fruit and left full underneath its tree. Soon after the sun hit in earnest, I stopped talking in order to focus all my energy on picking. By noon, when, as we learned later, the temperature was 120 degrees, I had stopped even thinking. Just raise arm, grasp cot, lower arm, place cot. Fill one lug, go get another. And still the trees stood full before us.

[ 66 ]

Someone called for a lunch break and Annie went into town for cold drinks. We gathered near the water faucet under a tree to eat the lunch we had brought with us.

The sun passed its peak, sweat continued to stream down my back and face, the lugs slowly filled. More than half the trees were picked, but our pace was slowing: would we be able to finish before dark? My fingers began to fumble, my arms and legs stopped doing what I asked. I began to have great respect for the professional picker, who picks day after twelve-hour day. How many lugs had I picked? I had tried to keep count. Eight? I began spending longer and longer at the water faucet between lugs. Still the trees beckoned.

By sundown we realized we had done all we could. In the few remaining hours of light, we counted the lugs, loaded them on the truck, paid our friends, and headed home. We had 125 lugs, two tons of juicy, delicious, aromatic fruit, and nine exhausted, sweaty, but triumphant ranchers.

The picking, of course, was just the beginning. Once back at the ranch, the lovely round cots had to be washed, sorted, cut, and placed on drying racks which Ranger had procured second-hand from a commercial dryer. That operation took forty-eight hours nonstop on tables set up in the fireplace room of the Big House, fueled by music from a stereo and its small portable generator. We placed the drying racks at a prepared space at the head of the garden, protected by fence from hungry cows and by screen from hungry birds and insects. After ten days of sun we moved the racks inside for another three weeks of dry shade. By then the pink and orange hemispheres had become brown and purple wrinkled discs that tasted delicious. We bagged them, put away a generous supply for ourselves, and sold the rest on consignment to our nearby health food store.

The venture was not a smashing financial success. After expenses, we made about $600, which was half of our monthly operating cost at that time. But we had put aside enough dried apricots to last us all winter, pulled off our first major project together, and garnered enough knowledge about the fruit industry to help us in our own orchard as well as in future drying operations of smaller scale.

Since we knew from the beginning that we were not here to make money, it was clear that living on the land meant simplifying and scaling down our needs as well as making ends meet with dollars when needed. When we made our first trip here, we brought with us a case of Triscuits, fifteen tins of Constant Comment tea, a case of Laura Scudders peanut butter, a case of ketchup, another of Saffola mayonnaise, dozens of loaves of wheatberry bread and English muffins from the day-old bread store. It didn't take long for the simplifying to begin. We stopped buying and started making bread within the first month; when the Triscuits and Constant Comment ran out, we never replenished the supply. One by one, the other items disappeared from shopping lists or were replaced by cheaper bulk brands. That original list is so different from the items that currently line our shelves that more recently arrived ranchers think we made it up to taunt them.

When my personal savings ran out within the first year, I was faced with trying to live with no private money at all, a situation which was to continue for three years until I started making small sums with magazine writing. All of my real survival needs — including such items as stamps, toothpaste, and Tampax — were provided out of the ranch operating budget, but there was no money for a milkshake from town, for a special book I might want, or for a needed article of clothing.

I looked forward to the $25 my parents sent at Christmas and my birthday to fill in some of the empty spots, learned to recycle my clothes from the health food store free box, and took out a library card. My real needs that fell outside the ranch budget were mysteriously provided for: a visitor left a pair of winter boots just my size and told me to keep them when I called it to her notice; a friend of a friend said he had been looking for a good home for his old backpack (a piece of equipment I needed for our camp work) and would I like it?; through an acquaintance in the city I was able to buy a brand new $150 down sleeping bag for $25, sold cheap because it was a trial model. I will stop just short of suggesting that the universe will provide similarly for anyone in real need who has faith in its benevolence, but I must add that at no time before or since, when I've had money, have such gifts come my way. In fact, the week after I received my first $50 check for a magazine piece, my dog Jessica, who never needed medical attention when I couldn't afford it, somehow managed to get an infected foot which required $45 of vet work to heal. I paid joyfully.

In March of our second year, Allen, the foreman of the 30,000 acre cattle and horse ranch six miles to the north of us, asked if we'd be interested in hauling his 200 tons of hay the thirty miles from town past our place to their barn. I have often wondered, now that I realize that hauling hay is not an occupation for amateurs, why he — who certainly knew that — decided to give us a chance. If I didn't know him so well I might suspect it was a misguided desire to watch us dump load after load of hay onto the long and winding county road. Perhaps the real reason was that his normal hay haulers had fallen through and he was desperate. Or maybe it was just a crazy idea.

I have wondered just as often if we knew what we were doing when we said yes. I know I didn't. But then I remembered the gleam in Annie's eyes at the thought of driving a twenty-foot flatbed bobtail truck with ten gears and a split rear axle, and I think of Bruce devising ever new and better ways to stack the hay so it would make a steady load, and Michael tying trucker's knots that he prided himself on never slipping — and I guess that others did have some glimpse of the adventure ahead.

But no one could possibly have guessed the number of salt tablets we would swallow to make our way through the unbelievable summer heat, or the hours it might take to drive a loaded truck with a faulty radiator up the mountain road, or the bone-deep weariness that would make us fall into bed day or night after our runs, to catch a few hours of sleep before the next. Nor could we have guessed the feeling of accomplishment, the respect we finally irrevocably won from the neighbors, or the often electric communication with one another. Hay hauling will forever symbolize one phase of our lives together, and it stands almost by itself at the head of the summers we did it. When I think back, it might be today. . . .

*Dream:* I am at the river with Ashley. I see us sitting along the bank from afar. Suddenly there is a roar, and in horror we see a wave of tidal proportions rounding the last curve and heading toward the cove in which we sit. And then I am awake, some dim part of my consciousness identifying the horn of the hay truck signaling me that the loading crew is up from town and it's time for the unloaders, of whom I am one, to take over.

Though the sun is off the meadow and creeping up the hills across the river, my bedsheets are wet with perspiration from the day's heat. I am still groggy from this afternoon nap, which must serve as my night's sleep.

After ten days straight of round-the-clock hay hauling, I have not yet learned to take my necessary sleep easily in the daylight, and I doubt that I ever will.

I force myself up from bed, reach for my jeans and long-sleeved shirt, still grimy with dust and sweat from their last use. More out of habit than because it will do any good, I brush my hair and tie it back from my face. It is still beastly hot. I have a moment of compassion for the loading crew, who worked during the heat of the day in town. The horn honks again from the road. Grabbing my work gloves and a heavier shirt for the cooler night ahead, I leave the yurt and cross the meadow.

At the Big House, the loading crew — Michael, Deborah, Susie, and Russell — are drinking beer (a treat from town) and iced tea. As I check the bulletin board to see who else is signed up for the evening unloading, Bruce and Ashley walk in. It's only the three of us tonight; we usually aim for four on a crew, but the unrelenting heat is taking its toll on our energy, so an occasional three-person crew gives someone else a little longer recovery time. We try to do three complete runs a day, both loading and unloading, but forces beyond our control — overheated truck, unwieldy bales — often bring it closer to two.

Despite the heat, the back-breaking work, the mechanical hassles, and the uneven record of sleep, somehow hay hauling is a party. That spirit sets the tone as the crew for this run enthusiastically consumes quantities of bean salad, peanut butter and fresh bread, apples, iced tea, and water as we stand around the big chopping table in the kitchen.

"How's the load?" Ashley asks.

"Two hundred bales, seventy pounds each. Seems to be secure but leaning a little to the left. I checked the ropes at the bridge, so they should be okay. The truck overheated three times coming up. You'll need to take

[ 71 ]

more water." Michael somehow manages to consume two pieces of bread with peanut butter and half an apple without missing a word.

Bruce asks Deborah how she is feeling. This was her first run since a ninety-pound bale landed square on her head last week while she was working in the barn, placing the unloaded bales. She sat down hard and saw stars for an hour or two and couldn't turn her head without pain until yesterday. Our cowboy friends said she was lucky to remember her name after a knock like that; they clearly were impressed with her determination to get back to work as soon as she could operate her neck.

"I'm okay," she says in response to Bruce's question. "But I'll be glad to get to bed tonight." Susie groans in assent.

Taking an apple for the road, Bruce, Ashley, and I gather our things and step out into the fresh night air. The nearly full moon is up, the sky turning fast to dark, the stars just beginning to find their way through. This is why I prefer the night runs despite my interrupted sleep, I think. Look at this night. They only come like this in summer, and I wouldn't miss it for anything.

The moon highlights the big yellow truck, loaded with hay and settled incongruously at the road overlooking the silent meadow. It looks like a mechanical monster of a banana slug or perhaps a misplaced item from a science fiction feature. It is so out of place that somehow the rest of the world is transformed to encompass it, and in my mind this bucolic scene becomes a surrealistic still life.

Bruce pulls on the ropes that strap the bales to the truck, tightens a knot here and there, then climbs into the driver's seat. Ashley gets in next to him, and I sit on the outside. We check behind the seat for hay hooks, replace the refilled water jugs, and hang onto our gloves. A split second before Bruce turns the key, I hear a coyote call from across the river, but then it is done, and the roar of the motor obliterates all other sound from the night.

It takes thirty minutes to drive from our place to the Horse Ranch barns in a car. In a truck loaded with seven tons of hay, it takes at least an hour, more if we need to stop when the truck overheats. Bruce drives slowly, in second low gear, feeling the sway of the load behind.

The cab carries us high off the road. The windshield stretches almost to my knees and wraps around the side of my vision. There is no hood between me and the road, and the ride is smooth and easy. I can see and feel the yellow lights that outline the truck, feel the bridled power of the big engine carrying us along. The night is still, no wind to move the trees, no wildlife visible to disturb the impression of gliding past a vast still life. I seem to watch us from far away.

My reverie is interrupted by Bruce and Ashley's talk. It's one of their favorite reels: what we will do when we take over the county (legitimately, that is, by getting our people elected to office).

Ashley: "What are we gonna do about all those hippies on welfare?"

Bruce: "Put 'em to work planting trees, tearing out those awful super-highways and making roads in their place."

Ashley: "But what about the tourist dollars?"

Bruce: "Tourists? We want the county to be good for people to live in."

And so on. It can and does and will go on forever. I lapse into my still life once more and watch the cut-out trees and cardboard bushes pass underneath the sequined sky.

Finally the tidy frame houses of the Horse Ranch pass by the windows, and then we arrive at the barn. Bruce eases the hay-toting monster through the gate, neatly avoids the mudhole in the middle of the barnyard, and backs into unloading position at the sliding door of the barn. He turns the key and we all pause for a moment of blessed silence before starting work. Ashley remembers to check the baling book, which records the number of bales on each load and often has little notes of advice or information from loaders to unloaders. He chuckles and then reads. "From Susie: 'June 25, 1973. We have now loaded the equivalent of a large herd of elephants onto the truck and driven it from Daytona Beach, Florida, to Cleveland, Ohio.'"

We jump down from the truck to reassign our portion of the elephant herd to its resting place for the winter. We work systematically, untying the ropes, coiling them, replacing them behind the seat in the truck cab. Ashley turns the switch to start the generator that operates the lights in the barn. Bruce and I place the conveyor belt unloader — which is powered by a small gasoline engine — in position, stretching from the truck gate to the barn loft.

I take my position on the truck end of the unloader; I will feed onto the belt the bales that Bruce hands me from where he stands farther up on the truck. Ashley stands at the other end of the unloader, in the barn, to pull the bales off the belt and stack them for the winter. Bruce starts the unloader and we begin.

I settle into the rhythm of the work: bend, hook, lift, unhook. The hay hooks by now feel like natural and efficient extensions of my hands, allowing me to move bales that are three-quarters of my weight and height with surprising ease. That feeling of natural extension, however, threatens to get me into the only real trouble I face in my position at the head of the unloader. Bend, hook, lift, unhook. If my timing is off, I sometimes miss the unhook, and my carefully placed bale ascends the conveyor belt with my hay hooks still embedded in its sides. My proper course of action then is to let go of the hooks — fast — or I, too, will ascend the conveyor belt, attached to bale and hooks. Letting go might seem to be a common sense reflex action, but in fact it feels so unnatural to relinquish my hold on the hooks that I must startle myself out of my new identity and make myself consciously give them up.

But tonight I'm having no such troubles with timing. Bend, hook, lift, unhook. I can hear Bruce breathing heavily near me and the thud of the bales as Ashley places them in the barn. The stars glow overhead, I am grateful for the cool of the night and enjoy the pull of muscles in my body. Then, suddenly, the rhythm is broken. Sputter, sputter, pop, the unloader stops. "Recreational vehicles," Ashley mutters, pulling out the current favorite in his repertoire of obscenities.

We all climb down to take a look. What could be the matter? Out of gas? Nope. Something caught? Not that we can see. Out of balance? Nope. Bruce goes on a bit about how helpful machines are, always there when you need them, and then it's clear that we will have to wake Allen for help. I have never been enthusiastic about waking people in the middle of the night. I bequeath the task to the boys and lie back on the hay to watch the stars.

We met Allen early in our first summer. He is a tall, strong man with three grown daughters, who wears a ten gallon hat as if he was born in it and sits a horse as easily as he walks. But it didn't take long to see that there was much more to him than the Marlboro man image he projects. Back when we were still getting to know him, he and Michael had a long talk one day about the wildlife around us. Allen spoke at length about the big cats — mountain lions — who still roam these hills.

"You know, Michael," he said with a funny look in his eye, "there's nothing like the feeling you get after a long chase, to finally look up there in a tree and see that big cat just waiting for you to shoot him."

[ 75 ]

Michael fell right into the trap. "You mean you *kill* mountain lions?" he gasped, appalled.

"Kill them?" Allen echoed. "Heck no, I shoot them with a camera. Got reels and reels of film up at the house. You should come and take a look at them sometime."

Lying there on the hay and listening to the tree frogs, I realize we have never taken him up on that invitation. I tuck it in the back of my mind to remind him of sometime, as I hear three pair of footsteps coming toward me. Bruce, then Ashley and Allen come into view.

"Hello, Barbara," Allen says. "What are you doing up at this hour?" His wrinkled shirt and sleepy face indicate that the question is really directed at himself. Flashlight in hand, he examines the small engine, muttering under his breath. Bruce and Ashley know enough to keep quiet, but I try to make up for his having had to get out of bed with some silly small talk that finally, blessedly, runs out of its own accord. Allen doesn't seem to notice particularly, but he does appreciate the fact that this is a party.

"Crescent wrench," he's saying. "Where do you think I'd find a crescent wrench? Thirty thousand goldarned acres, and I still can't find a crescent wrench when I need one." A comment to make us feel right at home, if we didn't already. We follow him into a shed, the comfortable clutter of which strikes another familiar note. Bruce and Ashley are giggling at some private joke about the nature of human beings. Allen needs no explanation and joins in the laughter.

He pokes around on the worktable, through the shelves, in the toolbox. Suddenly there is a gleam in his eye and his strong arm reaches across a bench and comes up with — the crescent wrench. Waving it over his head like a conquering warrior, he leads our little troupe back to the barn.

A few turns of the wrench and replacement of a bolt with another he had pocketed in the toolshed, and the unloader is puttering away again in the night air, which by now is completely charged with summer electricity. Allen decides against returning to bed. "Think I'll give you a hand to finish this, now that I'm up," he says.

Allen joins Ashley in the barn. With renewed energy, we swing the bales from one to another, up the conveyor belt, from arm to arm again, and finally into place. The pile on the truck slowly shrinks and the stack in the barn grows in proportion. I feel something personal for each bale that passes through my hands. Bend, hook, lift, unhook. The work continues, enlivened now and then by Allen's comments from the barn.

Last bale finally in place, Bruce and I shut off the unloader, grab the water jug, and climb up into the barn, where Ashley and Allen have already flopped onto the new hay. As we pass the water around, Allen, prompted by each of us in turn, tells stories. Stories of cattle and hay, of bears and wild boar, of the real untouched wilderness, where his heart truly lies. Through my early morning weariness, I hear not just his words but even more his tone of voice and the force of life behind the words. Here is a man who works hard for a living, whose livelihood depends on the many and varied moods of nature. How many other midnights has he been called from a warm bed because a heifer was having a bad calving or a truck had broken down ten miles away? If the season is bad, if there is not enough feed for the cattle, there is not as much profit at year's end.

But it is all right. He doesn't expect the days to pass smoothly, and he knows that it is all right. From his words rises that intangible feeling of partnership with the earth, of genuine love and compassion for life's creatures, of an abiding faith in the goodness of life. From his eyes, his voice, and his face shine the calm good humor of one who has met life directly, on its own terms, and found a place carved just for him. I realize how lucky I am to know him.

It is just beginning to get light in the east as Allen walks back into his house to start the day properly. I am covered with dust and hay; my scalp itches, my muscles ache, my jeans stick to my skin. Bruce climbs back into the driver's seat, Ashley next to him, I on the outside. We drive faster with the empty truck. By the time we park on the county road and blow the horn to wake the next crew, the stars have faded from the morning sky.

Hauling hay earned us $3000 toward the mortgage payment, but it also came at just the time the garden was being planted and other projects such as construction were beginning. The major efforts demanded by hay hauling left limited energy for those other projects that were a more integral part of our being here. The third summer we didn't finish the hay until ten days into summer camp. The overlap meant that we didn't get the garden planted in time and the vegetables got off to a slow start, from which they never recovered. That was a graphic reminder of the toll hay hauling was taking.

Then there was the injury list. By that third season, the following injuries were directly attributable to the hay: one broken wrist; one finger smashed in car door; three sprained backs; and two severe cases of hay-induced asthma. And Teresa, who had been a member of the ranch family since our second summer, lost a precious diamond ring.

But by that time, summer number four, we were already into a new phase of our economic structure, and hay hauling slipped quite naturally and only slightly tainted into its special place in ranch history. By then we had become a licensed foster home; summer camp led into full-time boarding school for nine teenagers and then into another camp the follow-ing summer. We expected that school and summer camp would complete the shift of the burden of economic support from individuals with money to the group as a whole. And, since the operation of a full-time alternative school had been one of our dreams from the beginning, we hoped finally to see our lives and our work merge more perfectly.

The stories of summer camp and school are in chapters IX and X, so I won't repeat them here. But these ventures marked a critical turning point in my life and in ranch life as well. It became clear before the school year was over that it was not going to answer our financial needs as we had hoped. Economic realities came crashing down. By then we had scaled our style of living down to the point that we spent only $1500 per person per year, excluding travel, but including land payments, both taxes and mortgage, and all operating and living expenses — yet we still had to lean on income from inherited capital to make it.

It was time to set up a financial system that would allow the personal flexibility required by our different interests and meet our needs at the same time. It was also time to share the responsibility of economic survival equally, regardless of personal resources.

After a great deal of thinking and talking, we drew up a budget whereby each adult in residence would pay $70 each month for operating expenses and an additional $1000 each year toward the mortgage pay-ment. The monthly budget breaks down into the follow categories:

food and household (matches, sponges, dish soap): $30.00 per person
livestock (feed and vet care for chickens and cows):  $8.00 per person
fuel (propane, kerosene, gasoline for ranch use):  $14.00 per person
machines (car, truck, tractor, chain saw upkeep): $13.00 per person
agriculture (seeds and tools):  $5.00 per person

The budget covers just bare minimum group expenses: those who have propane stoves in their own dwellings buy their own propane; people with pets (including horses) buy their own pet food; people with private vehicles maintain them with their own money: ranch-bought food is primarily staples such as flour, rice, oil, honey, and beans, and most of us supplement it with our own money.

I pay my monthly bill with my salary as a part-time research assistant for a local publishing company. Michael and Bruce secured a reforestation contract with the Department of the Interior that paid them for planting trees along our logged-over slopes. Carol is developing a tree nursery, Russell has a foundation grant for a book of his photography, Teresa takes freelance work as a systems analyst, and Susie has a part-time counseling job while she earns her family counseling license.

We have now made two mortgage payments and maintained the ranch for a year under this structure, long enough to assess some of its pluses and minuses. On the plus side, it is a clear sharing of the burden of operating the ranch in concrete terms, a real relief after years of depending disproportionately on those with inherited money. And it does accommodate our various drives to write books and to travel, as we had hoped, while still affirming our long-term commitment to the land and to each other.

But it also has resulted in some fragmentation of our energy and undermined long-term group projects, such as renovation of the Big House and expansion of the garden, and this probably will continue at least until our individual means of livelihood are more established. I fought that fragmentation very hard at first, but it seems inevitable to me now, a small part of the larger, more important process of figuring out how to maintain the ranch while we continue to grow and dream. My acceptance of that situation is perhaps my final coming to terms with the reality of money and its influence on the other choices of life.

I can still say with sincerity that the need for money does not dominate my life, nor does it determine ranch activity. Money has been one of a multitude of factors that have brought us to this stage, which is surely more of a beginning than an end. It's impossible to know whether or not our current financial arrangements will remain flexible enough to meet the challenges that lie ahead. The next bend is too far in the future to see just now. But having made it this far, with the difficult first years behind us, the odds are increasingly in our favor. The survival that was once a major question confronting us is more and more a basic assumption.

# VI

# Not Voting and
# Other Rituals

AFTER MY parents visited the ranch two years ago, they were asked to report to their church Sunday School class, which was studying living alternatives. Following their presentation — which included slides and an account of meeting a skunk in the meadow — the first question was, "But who's the boss?"

My father laughed and said that there wasn't one. He went on to explain that it was his impression that efficiency didn't rank in the top two or three of our priorities, and leadership had never really made a case for itself.

My father was right. Greater than any wish for smooth management or effortless decision making was our compulsion to make personal choices, including mistakes. The political experience of the sixties, which taught us that a new world could be built only by individuals willing to change their lives, confirmed whatever natural leanings toward anarchy I had. By the time we moved here, I had already realized that the only real discipline or progress had to come from within.

[ 83 ]

Idealistic and stubborn and young, we quickly found that it took time and patience to make decisions we could live with. In one of our earliest meetings that first summer, Bruce said that we were in trouble if we ever resorted to taking a vote in order to decide something. A vote, he said, was either temporary tyranny or a compromise that satisfies no one. A real solution to a problem demands a synthesis, not a compromise, and that process takes time and personal growth.

I remember only one time when we came close to voting. It was the first fall, and George and David, friends of ours from Palo Alto days, had been living at the ranch since mid-August. Hunting season opened over Labor Day weekend, and David suggested at dinner the following week that venison would add some nice flavor to our winter meals.

Since I had stopped eating meat a year before we moved to the ranch, I wasn't too excited about venison stew. And I had very strong feelings about hunting — I did not like it and was especially opposed to any hunting on this land. Though we had never discussed it, I just assumed that everyone else felt as I did. But George spoke up and said he also would like meat during the winter, and he felt that we should shoot it ourselves rather than go to a supermarket and buy a chunk that someone else had killed.

"Besides," David added, "I like to hunt. That's how I first learned about the woods. I still remember the smell of those early fall mornings when I was barely old enough to hold a gun."

There was an awkward silence. I was stunned, and felt a tidal wave of emotions washing over me. From the expressions on others' faces, I guessed I was not alone.

Carol spoke first, and eloquently, about wanting this land to be free from the violence of gunshots, to be a haven for the wild animals around. She wanted to live in harmony with nature and that meant no killing.

Ashley also had hunted during his boyhood. He answered Carol with some heartfelt eloquence about the feeling of the oneness of all creation, and especially of the transcendent connection between hunter and prey that unites them in a world of their own. "Do you know what it's like to pull the trigger and see the bullet connect?" he asked. "I love ducks, I really do — and I know that I love them more than anyone can who hasn't pulled that trigger."

George pointed out that hunting the deer was really good for them, anyway. Without our weeding out some of the bucks every fall, they would overpopulate this area and great numbers of them would have a slow and painful death by starvation each winter.

"How do we really know that?" Ranger asked. "The deer got along fine for hundreds of years before we came. Better to let nature find its own balance anyway. If we leave them alone they'll regulate their own numbers."

"But you can't ignore human influence on the whole process," George responded. "It's because we're here that the wolves aren't. We have a responsibility to try to right the balance we have upset, and hunting is one way. Besides, the Indians hunted."

"Yes, but they were themselves living in harmony with the land," Carol said. "Their consciousness was different than ours. We've lost that. We don't know how to kill from the center of oneness."

"How do you know unless you've tried it?" said Ashley. "How do you know what it's like for me?"

By this time the talk had grown emotional, and voices came loud and on top of each other. The knot in my stomach tightened and ached. Around the table faces were flushed, and I watched hands clench with feeling.

[ 85 ]

"If we were to hunt on this land, it would destroy my whole reason for being here," I said, my voice tight and quivering. "I don't want to hear gunshots. I don't want the deer or the squirrels to hear gunshots, or feel them. I want to live *with* the animals, not in pursuit of them." Tears were close, but I stopped talking in time.

"But, wait," David said. "You want the right to live on this land without gunshot. I want to be able to hunt and eat meat. Is your right greater than mine? Isn't that what you're saying?"

I could no longer think clearly; anger and emotion were crowding my thoughts. But I was more and more convinced that I was right, and George and David and Ashley, my good friends and part of my family, were wrong and bad. I felt passionately that hunting would be a betrayal of the land and the trust given to us.

Then someone suggested that we take a vote on a hunting policy for the land. I heard the suggestion with relief: I wanted a way to stop the discussion which had become so ugly, and voting seemed the only possible way out of the impasse that David had pinpointed. Others nodded, too, their faces showing similar feelings.

We had started around the table taking votes, when suddenly George said, "I don't believe it. This is the first time we have ever voted on anything. Do we want to set that kind of precedent?"

My immediate emotional reaction was "yes!" Clearly, I was going to "win" by a vote. But something in the question stopped me. It had the same effect on others, and I felt a pause sweep the table. It was clear that a vote at that moment wouldn't do any more than make a law. It couldn't possibly effect an agreement, a real expression of who we were and how we all wanted to live together. No synthesis was possible with feelings so aggressively polarized.

Frustrated and a little reluctant, we nevertheless backed off. We left the Big House still in turmoil, with no decision reached, but deep feelings imprinted on everyone's minds. The question hung in the air for days, but there was no more discussion.

And then somehow, in individual minds, a consensus was reached. George and David hunted on nearby public lands and our land was free from gunshot. (Ashley, it seemed, was never that interested in hunting here but was drawn into the hunters' "side" of the argument on principle.) This was a solution that no one had been able to think of in the heat of the discussion, and it is a true synthesis of our feelings that continues as policy to this day.

That is how it happens, and the process of not voting has become a ritual for us now, a ceremonial reflection in the tradition of an Indian council of how we live and grow together. A subject comes up, usually in murmur of twos or threes at first, then we will all sit down to talk. We decide nothing, and everyone leaves the meeting feeling very frustrated and fed up with meetings. And then in a day or two we all realize that a decision has been reached after all, and we all know what it is, though no one can say exactly how. Not efficient perhaps, but effective, if what you want most is real harmony and a chance for personal growth. Harmony and personal growth *do* rank at the top of our priorities, and the older we get, the more naturally efficient that harmony seems to be.

In the same way that decision making is a process with a mythic dimension rather than a mundane task, so it is with other basic facts of our lives. Living here transforms many of our simple daily and seasonal habits into rituals. That has been true from the very first weeks, when we noticed that anything that was done more than twice became imbued with a touch of ceremony. Meals, mail time, wood cutting, collecting the eggs — all became ritual acts of a sort. In the beginning our eyes were especially glazed with magic, and not all of those mini-rituals have endured, but the feeling of richness and fullness that is at the heart of ritual persists and is clearly deeper than the projection of any starry-eyed neophyte in the country.

This is a life of palpable richness. The sensation comes directly from nature, whose daily and seasonal cycles evoke the greater rhythms of life and death, fullness and diminution, light and dark. Sunrise and set, the growth and diminishment of the moon, the ebb and flow of the seasons are all nature's rituals. They are powerful images, as well as determining daily realities to those like us who live far from the artificial conveniences of electricity, central heating, and grocery stores.

We also live without television and movie theatres. And like many others who have been in that situation, we tell stories. Constantly, and over and over, to anyone who will listen. We use visitors and newcomers as an excuse, but it is clear that those who enjoy the stories most already know the words by heart.

Remember when Ranger bought Annie a baby pig named Mudslide for their anniversary, only to wake up one night three months later (when the piglet was closer to the size of a young horse) and see it on the end of their bed, snoring peacefully? Remember the Big Freeze, when all the water pipes burst (because we, like most of our neighbors, had not antici-pated below-freezing temperatures that night and had forgotten to leave the taps running)? We had to carry water by hand for cooking, dishwash-ing, and bathing for three winter weeks until we completed repairs of the plumbing. Then there was the kidnapping from the first summer, the time the camp kids tore the steps off the second story of the White House (which served as camp headquarters), and the night the FBI came to visit. And how about the day a 250-pound visitor fell off a horse on the other side of the river, far from a road or even a helicopter landing area? We had to carry him on a stretcher fashioned from a door for two miles through the brush and up the hills to the closest spot an ambulance could reach, thinking with each jarring step that his back was broken. (It wasn't, but he did have three cracked ribs.)

The stories we tell most often are those that make fools of us. For a group of supposedly intelligent, well-brought-up, reasonably capable human beings, we have an amazing collection of embarrassing stories. Remember when the white truck rolled into the pond, not once but twice in two months? Or how about the time David got the Caterpillar stuck while trying to drain the pond and had to call in all the local Cat drivers for advice on how to get it out of the watering hole? And who could forget the time one of our budding mechanics tried to thaw the frozen fuel line of the same white truck with the acetylene torch? (Luckily, it didn't work, and he lived to tell the story.)

Picture a cold winter evening in late November. We are gathered at the Big House and dinner is just over. Carol and Bruce and I get up to clear the table. Michael, Susie, Ranger, and Deb drift into the fireplace room and pull the tattered green couch closer to the fire. The children are playing horse with notable sound effects in their playroom off the dining area. Ashley, Mark, and Kathleen linger over a last cup of coffee around the table.

Outside the rain is pouring down, and the sound is loud on the tin roof. No moon tonight. No one is in a hurry to leave the warmth of the Big House and venture forth to a cold dark cabin. Bruce gets out the chess game and sets it up for himself and Ashley. Deb comes out to help Carol and me with the dishes and wait for the tea water to boil. In the fireplace room we can hear that Ranger has picked up his guitar.

Susie and Michael are talking about publicity for next year's summer camp. They agree that we need to find a way to contact the people we would really like to reach. Bruce, catching a word or two from the other room, says "Yeah — no more kids whose parents just want to get rid of them for a few weeks. Let's get some kids who really want to be here." Ashley agrees. "We aren't in the policeman business, after all," he says.

That's all it takes. Suddenly Michael is off and running with summer camp stories, interrupted now and then by Susie or Bruce for correction or elaboration. Deb returns with the teapot, in time to chime in with a story or two of her own, and before long Ranger puts down his guitar because he's laughing so hard.

Dishes done, I turn off the hot water heater, pour myself a cup of tea, and join the family. The light from the fire illuminates the faces clustered in the old pine-paneled room. In the other room the children evidently haven't gotten sleepy yet — their game continues at a healthy decibel level. Here, plans for next summer — which is, after all, still months away — seem to have been completely forgotten as one story leads to another, and then another, and the laughter drowns out the sound of the rain outside.

Some stories have been told so many times that they have achieved near mythic proportions. Especially when one of these comes up again, and especially on a night like this, I realize the importance the stories play in our lives, the sense of almost epic meaning and connection they impart. Storytelling somehow makes who we are and what we are doing real, in the very ways that matter most. The fire slowly burns down, and we finally rise to make our separate ways through the darkness to our beds. But the blackness seems not quite so thick now, and the storm not so intense. The stories wrap themselves like a warm muff around my rain-soaked clothes and fortify me against the cold and lonely night, both within and without.

Then there are the rituals that come not from the land, but from our cultural and religious heritage: birthdays, Halloween, Thanksgiving, Easter, Christmas. We celebrate them all, mixing our separate childhood traditions with new elements of our own devising.

The winter solstice, which is also Russell's birthday, is the day we choose our Christmas tree from the stands of young trees on the land that need to be thinned. This year we are only five on the ranch, for the others are involved in various trips to town and pre-Christmas city activities, but tradition holds. We five — Michael, Bruce, Russell, Kathy, and I — will perform the tree-cutting ritual. There is a feeling of festivity in the air.

First, birthday breakfast in bed for Russell, with special treats: scrambled eggs, English muffins, last summer's blackberry jam, and orange juice. We all join in the celebration until it is gone and we can eat no more. Then, bellies full, bow saw in hand, we set off to the woods.

The day is clear, fresh with the smell of yesterday's rain. As we enter the forest, we look back to see the horses scattered about the meadow, drying off in the sun. There is an unmistakable air of well-being about; the sky is as blue as summer, and the bird songs seem to come from the heart of spring. But the wind, the temperature, the heavy moisture, and our purpose maintain December's hold on us.

We are in high spirits. Choosing a Christmas tree has many associations for all of us: all those other Christmases of our growing up come rushing at us, and memories fly wild in that childlike feeling of anticipation that glows shyly from behind our grown-up eyes. We fall into pantomime and pretend we are in a Christmas tree lot on a city street corner. "How 'bout this nice silver one, Harriet?" "Lower prices 'round the corner, I hear." "Now, Charley, let's get a nice *little* one this year, one that will fit on the coffee table in front of the bay window."

Michael has in mind a plump pine sapling from a cluster that needs to be thinned along the road to Orr's land. Russell wants a *big* one. I remind him that it always looks bigger when we get it in the house, and recall that we invariably have to trim our forest vision to living room size when we get it inside. He says that's just what his mother always says. The rest of us have no pictures in our heads, except that it should be healthy and bushy and just right.

We veer off the path, right into the fullness of the woods. We are surrounded by trees, beautiful trees: oak, madrone, bay laurel. Their leaves shine with the moisture left from the rain. And stands of Douglas fir and ponderosa pine. Russell fancies that they duck their branches when they see us coming, pulling in their limbs along one side to appear imperfect enough to escape the saw. We respond with grim chuckles, not entirely comfortable with our role as nature's henchmen.

Michael spies a mushroom, rust-stained top with cream-colored gills, that he wants to give Deborah for Christmas. My black dog, Jojo, finds something to eat in a decaying branch.

Then suddenly, there it is: a tall fir, bushy, a perfect one, in a plot that needs thinning. We agree without discussion. Michael hands me the mushroom while he saws the trunk close to the ground. I think how well we have chosen, how happy the others will be.

Russell catches the tree as it falls, and raises the trunk to his shoulder. Bruce steps into the fullness of the branches to grab the middle, and

Michael follows because it looks like fun. Michael's and Bruce's heads are completely buried in the branches; the whole thing resembles the horse-costumed clowns in the circus — a strange, top-heavy creature with one head, six legs, and numerous waving green arms. Russell has to be the eyes for all six legs; he calls out the obstacles but — whether by design or not — never quite in time for Michael and Bruce to miss them. Russell steps over a fallen log, calls out "log!" just as Bruce is falling over it and Michael is about to. They zigzag through the forest, over, under, and through thick brush, large rocks, and tangled branches, their legs coming out every possible way from the fir boughs, Russell's head bobbing unconcernedly at the fore. Michael and Bruce, gasping with giggles, try impossibly to maintain the forward motion. Kathy and I are laughing too hard to be any help.

Then, abruptly, in the fraction of a second, by spontaneous unspoken accord, laughter turns to melody, and the woods are filled with three male voices singing "Silent Night." Without a word, the comedy is transformed. I feel a hush come over me, an awesome hush that the forest seems to share. For an instant the woods shimmer before my eyes in unexpected tears. It happens so easily, the mood slips in and out of itself, life turns a new angle, we move around the circle. Laughter turns to prayer, parade turns into procession. We sing our way home, in the wake of a fir tree carried gently as a virgin.

[ 93 ]

# VII

# "Our Lives Feel Like a Slow Earthquake"

NATURE'S mood has turned again. The sunny clarity that marked the end of December has become a rawness that is stark and passionate. The trees on the hillside are bare, stripped of leaves, naked skeletons that groan in harsh January winds. The stream is loud with new rain, swelled to overwhelming proportions, roaring down the rocky gorge. The days are gray and tumultuous.

Letter from a friend: "Our lives feel like a slow earthquake. We're holding on to see what the lay of the land looks like when it all settles." I know just what he means. That feeling of having no solid ground beneath us has prevailed since early in our first summer, product of our ages, the age, our choices for our lives, and God knows what else. I don't think it was this way for everyone, but for me that first wave of crisis was an unlooked-for shock. But even then, even as I fought against it, I could taste the inevitability and the vitality of what was happening. There was something real at the heart of the earthquake, but my own efforts to make

[ 95 ]

sense of it — quickly, of course, so it would stop — were frustrated time and again as one familiar landmark after another seemed to be swept away.

By the first fall, the pace of the crises had slowed somewhat, and for our own emotional survival, we learned to distance ourselves from the turbulence periodically and to call on new sources of support from each other and the land. But controlling the earthquake into submission was beyond our power — and we didn't want to anyway.

I managed to escape the devastation of a personal crisis until the spring of our third year. Up until then I saw change as a mostly collective phenomenon, a vital avenue of political and personal growth that challenged my preconceptions and emotions and that mostly stayed within limits I could handle. Change itself was a principle I believed in; and if it was uncomfortable or even downright exhausting from time to time, still the very obvious positive results in terms of personal growth (breaking down of old prejudices, development of greater wisdom and maturity, compassion) left me no doubt that "living on the edge," as we called it, was exhilarating and, beyond any question, the way I wanted my life to be.

Then the relationship in which I had invested heart and soul for the previous three years fell apart. My first reaction was total disbelief. I refused to accept it. I was sure that the depth of love that I felt, and that I knew he felt too, had to be true. And if true, had to be possible. Surely there was nothing stronger or more beautiful than the force of that love, which had awakened realms of feeling and inspiration within me that I had never known before. It simply couldn't be over. That would mean that most of the feelings and ideas which had seemed so real and true during those three years were false, or at least terrifyingly inadequate. I could no longer trust my perceptions. I felt the world slip away around me, and I plunged into the longest, darkest tunnel I had ever known.

I awoke in the cold hours before dawn unable to sleep, despair clawing at my breast. My heart palpably ached; each breath hurt. I lurched between anguish that tore me apart in deep gasping sobs and anger so violent that its intensity terrified me. I went through my days in a trance, determined not to break down completely. I hardly remember anything about what I did for those weeks — all of my vital essence was withdrawn and concentrated on a desperate attempt to survive. Part of that effort was an irrational grasping at straws of explanation: why had this happened, what did it mean? But my struggles to make sense were frantic and panic-stricken, not the stuff that real understanding comes from. Gone were any romantic notions of the exhilaration of living in flux, of the beauty of change. This was a crisis that overwhelmed me. It was too much.

The days stretched into weeks, and then a month and more. Finally, just barely, I felt the darkness tremble. I found myself able to sense, if ever so slightly, something beyond the horrible nightmare that had turned me into a walking zombie. Though I was still too upset to be very conscious, I was dimly aware of a pinpoint of light, way down deep within, that agitated for expression. Somewhere down there I was intact, and healthy, and sane — and I wanted to break out of the darkness in which I had nearly lost myself.

It was in that frame of mind — still distraught, but struggling toward health — that I decided to attend a weekend seminar a few hours' drive from here. It had been so long since I had wanted to do anything at all that I fanned that glimmer of interest into a spark that evoked preparations for a real trip. I carefully selected a wardrobe of city clothes, did the preparatory reading for the seminar, and arranged to borrow Sweet Pea, the ranch's '51 Chevy sedan. Bathed and perfumed and dressed in clean long skirt and sweater, I felt a great rush of freedom. As I drove past the cattle guard and down the muddy county road, I realized that this was the first time I'd been off the ranch, or wanted to be, for two months.

I rehearsed my little litany for getting through the day. Think about *now*, I told myself, maybe as far in the future as this afternoon, but on no account let next year enter your mind. And the past is forbidden territory. It has happened; it doesn't matter why, or who was wrong, or if there is anything to do about it now to make it different. It has happened. All that matters is to accept it, take a deep breath, and get on with life.

Brave words, and they worked for almost half the drive to town. The feeling of freedom made it easy, and I found a surprising exhilaration in watching the changing scenery and in steering Sweet Pea skillfully around the mountain curves that I knew like an old cheerleading routine. Somewhere past the summit I recognized the return of the dull ache in my stomach and the occasional invasion of my mind by one of the forbidden questions. But I was determined to be in control of this weekend, and succeeded in allowing the unwanted thoughts and emotions to occupy only a distant corner of my consciousness.

By the time I pulled into town, I was tired from the effort but pleased that I was holding my own. I decided to treat myself to a nice lunch at the local health food restaurant.

Getting Sweet Pea into a parking place wasn't nearly so easy as guiding her down the mountain, but after my second try, she nestled peacefully at the curb. I ran a comb through my hair, checked it in the rearview mirror, and thought how comforting it was not to have to lock the doors. A low crime rate was one of the virtues of this little town, and besides, I would be able to keep an eye on Sweet Pea from the window while I ate.

I chose a table near the front and was looking over the menu, which I was gratified to see hadn't changed at all during the time I had been out of circulation, when I heard my name called. It was Marilyn, an acquaintance from town who was a born-again Christian. I hadn't seen her for months and asked her to join me.

She was radiant, and happy to see me. "It's been a long time," she said. "How are you?"

My tough resolve melted before the realization that she really wanted to know. "Well, to tell you the truth," I answered with a catch in my voice, "I'm not great. I've been having sort of a rough time for a month or two." I filled her in on a few of the details and told her what a hard time I was having accepting what had happened.

"Well, that's wonderful," she said when I finished.

I stared at her. "It is?"

"Sure," she continued. "Pain is God's way of calling you to Him. The more you hurt, the faster you get there. You are very lucky."

I considered that for a few minutes. I am generally a person who looks for the best in most situations, and I had already realized that some good was coming out of this unlooked-for pain. I felt chastened and a little wiser, and I was determined to emphasize whatever else that was good that I might find. But to see all that had happened as "wonderful," as something to be grateful for, as if this was really a preferable situation to what had been before — that was a little much. For a moment I felt again all the anger, the bitterness, the overwhelming sorrow. What was wonderful about that? No, I couldn't in any way feel that God had *wanted* that; it was too bad.

[ 99 ]

Still, it was nice to talk to someone who didn't know the other people involved very well and who could have cared less about the details. I was unendingly grateful for the shoulders and ears of my friends at the ranch, for the sympathy and righteous anger and unfailing support when I desperately needed it — but it was refreshing now to talk with someone who wasn't nearly so interested in giving me sympathy as in celebrating the meaning of what had happened and praising God for it.

Marilyn told me about the prayer group she had just started in town and of the healing that some of its members had experienced. She quoted Bible verses and shared with me some of her recent personal grapplings with faith. Through it all, she looked into my eyes with compassion and excitement. Her caring and sincerity made me feel good, regardless of whether I could accept all she said.

I was not attracted to the evangelical style of the local "born-again" churches. But God did matter to me and He was an important part of my life. So although some of Marilyn's words and the intensity of her emotions were beyond me, I did understand what she was talking about and felt a comforting kinship with her. Maybe there was a point to all this pain after all.

We were so engrossed in talking that I hardly noticed that most of the other people in the restaurant had left. But then the waitress came to clear our plates and I realized that I'd better get back on the road if I was going to reach the seminar site before dinner. So we quickly finished our sandwiches, paid the bill, and went out into the cool afternoon air.

"Well, thanks," I said in parting. "It's been really good to talk with you."

"I enjoyed it, too," Marilyn responded. "Bye, I hope things get worse for you," she added with a twinkle in her eye.

And sure enough, they did. After a fulfilling and relaxing weekend at the seminar, where I found I could indeed still concentrate and that I did after all have some interests outside myself, I returned to the ranch feeling mildly euphoric. That feeling lasted for a day, then two, and almost three before I plunged into depression once again. This time it seemed even worse, since I had been hoping that my several days of good spirits had meant the darkness had really passed. But the depression was once again undeniably real, even though it now seemed to come in cycles, interspersed with suspicious highs. I was beginning to get genuinely worried about myself, and a distant corner of my mind considered whether I might be turning into a manic depressive as I continued to pick myself up and then plunge to the depths again and again.

The plunging was mostly private, but my ranch friends knew me too well not to see what was happening. Concerned, they suggested that maybe I should go away for a while, take a trip, go to the city, get involved in something new and totally absorbing. I recognized that those were the recommended courses of action in cases such as mine, but I just didn't want to take any of them. I had no urge to leave, no place else that seemed any more attractive to me. I didn't want to meet new people or try a new activity. I didn't want to "get away." I wanted peace, and meaning, and a sense of harmony with the universe once again. And I wanted that right here, in this place that was so completely home for me.

In my despair, I turned to nature, my old trusted friend. The land had been there for me so many times, a soothing, constant presence, easy and accessible, a source of strength and clarity. I began a series of long walks in the rain and cold and intermittent sun, to the river, through the forest, over the hills. The exercise was good, but the easy comfort I had hoped for was not there.

Instead, the turbulence I felt inside was reflected around me. I found a mouse drowned and floating in the flood waters of the creek, its body bloated with death. I watched a tall fir tree crash to earth and lie trembling, rain water having washed the life-giving earth from its roots. In the hills I came upon the carcass of a deer, dead for not more than a day or two, its ribs protruding from the undernourished flesh. The spider who had kept me company for months in the yurt suddenly disappeared, probably gone away to die in the cold.

That wasn't what I wanted. I looked further, and noticed that the grass was sprouting green in the meadow and the salmon were once again laying their eggs upstream. The streams rushed ever stronger to the now-raging river, the hawks soared in the morning sky, and the sun continued to rise, now often behind clouds of rain. I ached for some answers, for it all to make sense, for something to fit into place. But everywhere I looked I saw more that didn't. Life, death, change, growth. And then again.

No soft answers, and no easy comfort. But each day I noticed that the sun would rise again. And that the same rain that drowned the mouse fed the grass and carried the salmon. The deer who died became food for the earth, and the bushes nearest her body would bear fruit next summer, perhaps for the nourishment of her fawns of the previous spring. No soft answers, but deep connections. An ebb and flow, life and birth, a rhythm whose evenness kept time with the unfailing rising of the sun. A force of life connections that transformed the little dyings into a chain of life. Or a force of deaths that claimed each birth in turn. But the truth was, there seemed to be no end, neither in life nor death. The duality contradicted itself, and completed itself, and rose through the absurd to something else.

Something else. That was what I wanted. And though I could deduce it, observe its effects, even almost sense it, I knew I did not know it. I returned from my walks with a glimmer of truth that was not mine.

I still can hardly look back upon this time without an involuntary shudder. I can remember all too easily that horrible feeling of panic, of the world cracking at the edge, and the black, sinking feeling in my stomach each morning when I would have to realize again that it was all true. I wanted to hide away, to die, to disappear. I wanted it to be all right again. I wanted the dreadful ache to go away. And most of all I wanted to break through. That was the way I phrased it to myself. The phrase came more from the physical sensation of my unbalanced condition than from some idea of what the cure might be. That physical sensation was very vivid: I felt tied up and imprisoned in a large black room, the walls of which were slowly but resolutely compressing. At the same time there was a sensation of steadily escalating pressure from inside me — so that I felt trapped and suffocated between pressure from both within and around me. Without knowing how or even really connecting up the images, I desperately wanted out, wanted to break through that black room into the light.

I simultaneously ran from and wanted to meet the inexorable pressure. And so the days passed, and I became more outwardly in control, though still highly disturbed inside. I cast about for books that might help me understand and push beyond the darkness I felt encased in. One afternoon I was reading the *CoEvolution Quarterly* when some words from a review by Stewart Brand leaped off the page: "It's always a shock to find that God doesn't care about your pain."

Something caved in in my stomach. What? I read it again. "It's always a shock to find that God doesn't care about your pain." Somewhere inside, part of the pressure turned to gas and made me lightheaded. What on earth does he mean? I wondered, grasping for some sort of rational explanation as the wave of dizziness threatened to engulf me.

God doesn't care about my pain? Wait a minute! What happened to God the Father of infinite compassion, God who loves the little sparrow, God who weeps for the prodigal son? God doesn't care about my pain? Then what is it — "it" meaning God, life, existence, the whole mess — all about?

Ignoring the light of truth that beeped from within me, I told myself that people will say all sorts of things to attract attention and who was Stewart Brand, anyway, that he should presume to know what God feels, and besides it just didn't make any sense.

But then — just as an intellectual exercise, mind you — I tried to figure out if it did. Let's see. God doesn't care about my pain. Well, then what does He care about? If He doesn't care about my pain, how can He care about my happiness? And if He doesn't care about my happiness, then what is life all about anyway? If not happiness?

Trying another approach, I remembered my conversation with Marilyn. "Suffering is the way God calls you to Him," she'd said. So He must care, I thought. And she'd added, "You are very lucky." I realized that I had begun to understand what she'd meant. There was a certain nobility of spirit that I had noticed in myself of late, and a new tolerance for and insight into the inevitable sorrow of life. I found a comforting empathy with those everywhere who were struggling with pain.

But wait a minute. "God doesn't care about your pain." "Pain is the way God calls you to Him." Suddenly I saw the link. Suffering is only — no

[ 105 ]

more than — a way that God calls you to Him. He doesn't care about the pain. He cares about you. About your being with Him.

And by the same reasoning, He doesn't in fact care about happiness. Happiness, sadness, joy, sorrow, ecstasy, pain: life, change, growth, death. None of it has any importance in itself, neither happiness nor pain, neither joy nor sorrow. Suffering — and happiness — are important only as a means to Something Else. God doesn't care about your pain, or your joy, or your money, or your hunger: He cares about you. He wants *you*. He wants me.

It was 2 a.m. several weeks later, nearly a year after my initial devastation. I was up late reading a book about World War II, which I thought that my generation ought to make an effort to understand, since it had shaken the world so deeply right before our entrance. Outside it was bitter cold, and my little fire needed constant feeding to keep the yurt comfortable. But I was so absorbed in the book that I kept forgetting to add more fuel, with the result that I had to wrap up in my down sleeping bag to keep my teeth from chattering. I huddled in one corner of my bed, close to the mantle lamp, as far as I could get from the dark.

The book was nearing its end, and the author was describing being in London and enduring a horrible strafing by Hitler's Luftwaffe. I was with her, down in the cellar, with strangers, without enough food or water or blankets. I was cold and scared, and nearly frantic because I didn't know where my husband was. The bombs dropped overhead. I heard the scream of the plane, the sickening screech of the falling bombs, and the shaking of the earth upon impact. Screams came from outside: where was my husband? Another woman in the shelter with me started to shriek out of mind-breaking terror. I heard another plane coming and braced myself for the possible collapse of the timbers above us which could mean that I would be buried alive.

And then, somehow, the terror exploded, the black box I had been living in for so long came apart, and I broke through. Suddenly, where for months there had been anger and pain and aching and fear — suddenly there was only awe. And I was enveloped in an overwhelming and transcendent humility, a humility so sweetly and completely transforming that I felt tears stream down my face. Suddenly, for the first time in this conscious life, I knew God, and knew myself in relation to Him. And there was nothing else. Nothing. No heartache, no pain, no struggle, no questions. Peace, joy, security, happiness — all were totally irrelevant. Nothing was left, absolutely nothing. Just God, and within Him, in true and complete relation, me. Which was everything. And still is.

# VIII
# On Eating Your Friends

ACORNS were a primary food source for the Indians who lived in these hills before me. Gathering them in the fall was a ritual that included the entire family, from the children who would climb the trees to shake down the nuts, to the grandmothers who helped pick the fallen nuts from the ground. With proper processing and storage, the acorns would last through the winter and into the spring and summer of the following year. Indian children, especially the girls, learned about the ways of oak trees as a natural part of growing up among them, part of the rites of survival that were handed down from grandmother to child, generation after generation.

Now I, who also have lived with oak trees most of my life in one place or another but never paid them much attention, am trying to learn what every Indian child knew. As I sit in my yurt in the shade of this majestic tree, which is just beginning to form little green acorns, and look out upon a hillside crowded with oaks, madrones, and firs, I am suddenly embarrassed that it has taken me so long. All at once I feel illegitimate living here like this and I sense that the trees have kept from calling it to my attention out of sheer politeness. I don't even know their names!

I turn first to books. There appear to be at least three different varieties of oaks here: black, white, and live oak. It is easy to pick out the black oaks with their sharply pointed leaves and fat dark acorns. Live oaks, too, are distinctive: they do not shed their leaves in winter, the leaves are shaped like holly, the acorns are long and slender. Then all the rest, by far the majority here, must be white oaks, right? That's what I conclude from the books, but I check with Andy to be sure.

Andy is the closest I come to having an Indian grandmother. He knows the land from the inside after years of living with it, and he knows how important it is to pass on his knowledge.

"So," I ask Andy on the last day of August of our second year, "do I have it right about the oaks?"

"Well, not exactly," is his slow reply. "Some of those that you're callin' white oaks are mush oaks. The Indians called 'em that because they made mush from the acorns. Mush oaks grow a lot faster than white oaks and their acorn is pointed. The white oak acorn is rounded at the tip. But you can't understand without seeing what I mean. Let's go take a walk."

Andy's lean, wiry body takes long strides through the grasses that are turning from brown to gray at the end of a long summer. I tag along just behind. As we walk he explains that we need to find trees with well-developed acorns to really see the differences, not an easy task this year because a late spring frost destroyed most of the flowers from which acorns develop. But he thinks we can find what we need. Along the way he points out the trees we pass. "This here's a mush oak, that's a white, there's a whole bunch of whites."

They all look the same to me. "How can you tell?" I ask. "Are you looking at the bark or the leaves or the shape?"

"They just look different to me," he says. "It all looks different. See,

those twigs are a little thicker, the leaves are different. But that's just gen-
eralizations. You'll see when we find some good examples."

We stop at a black oak and even though this is one I already know,
Andy takes out his pocket knife to cut a bunch of twigs, leaves, and acorns
so he can point out their special characteristics and we can use them for
comparison. "See the acorn, how fat it is. And the cap is particular, too.
Black oaks have little scales like fish."

This tree has acorns with little black marks on the nut. I ask if that is
another characteristic of black oaks. He says no, that those marks are the
special mark of this particular tree. If you know the trees well, you can tell
the exact tree an acorn comes from.

I am appropriately impressed. The Indians must have known the
trees like that, I think. And I get a glimpse of a time when people knew the
trees they lived among so well that they could tell by looking at a nut that
it fell from the big black oak over the hill and not from the one at the base
of the meadow. I remember what I have read about certain groves of oaks
belonging to individual Indian families, and I understand a little more of
the personal nature of the ties between human and tree.

We pass a multitude of mush oaks that, to my eyes at least, look just
like the white oaks in my books. Andy seems to be reading my thought. "I
saw a book once," he says, "which had a picture of a mush oak but they
called it a white oak. I don't know if the author didn't know the difference
himself or just got confused. But they're not the same." He reaches up to
cut off a sample of twigs, leaves, and acorns.

Andy is a careful teacher. We can't find exactly what he is looking for
— a single hillside with good specimens of all three varieties — but he
insists on finding trees that are typical enough of the species that I will be
able to see the differences among them for myself. Finally he finds a white

oak with acorns developed enough to be characteristic. He cuts down a small branch for me to handle. Comparing it with the mush oak, I can tell that the twigs of the white oak are thicker. Andy shows me that the white oak twigs also break more readily at the joints. A white oak will snap at its joints up to five or six years' growth, while a mush oak will snap only up to year three or four. "Of course," he adds, "since the mush oak grows so much faster, that doesn't necessarily help you much if you don't know what it is in other ways."

The leaves of both trees look about the same to me, though Andy says I will learn to tell them apart, but the acorns are definitely different, even to my untrained eye. The white oak nuts are a clear dome shape, while the ones from the mush oak always come to a point, although the size of the nuts varies somewhat from tree to tree. Andy says that the mush oak acorns have much less tannin; livestock can eat a good quantity safely, but just a few acorns from a white oak will make them sick.

I compare the two branches I am holding, being careful to keep the white oak in my left hand until I am sure I can tell it from the mush oak in my right. Andy lets me study them, knowing that his words are only clues to get me started and that I must make my own sense of it, feel the differences from the inside before I will really be able to tell on my own. "I think I've got it," I say at last. "You sure?" he says. And I know by the twinkle in his eye that I'll be quizzed the next time we meet.

As we walk back to the road, I ask him how he learned all this. From his father? He laughs. "No, my father wasn't born here. He came here late. They used to say that if my father had been a wild animal, he'd have starved. He didn't know these things." Andy pauses, thinking. "Just learned it from living here I guess. When you grow up in a place, you just kind of pick it up one way or another."

Once again I realized how late I am in starting. But ready, I think, to make up for lost time.

In a year like that, when a late spring frost had decimated the acorn crop, the Indians would have turned to buckeyes and last year's acorns for winter food. The buckeye is the first tree to lose its leaves as the season turns toward fall; it starts shedding greenery in August. The first autumn we were here, the falling leaves seemed so untimely that I was sure the buckeyes were all dying of some awful disease. But by the second year, I could laugh at myself and, instead of worrying, I watched for the large nuts that the bare branches divulged.

When the nuts turned shiny-brown and fell to the ground, I collected a basketful. Carefully following the directions I could find in books, I leached and ground the nutmeat, then roasted it lightly in the oven. And then, when I tasted it, I discovered why it was reserved for times of famine among the Indians. Even after careful processing, the meat was bland, pasty, and slightly bitter. I managed to make some of it into a sort of a cracker, and hoped for a good acorn crop another year.

The next fall the oaks were covered with little green nuts by late August. I read all I could find about gathering and processing them as the Indians did and quickly found that the books did not agree. But there was enough of a common thread that I judged myself ready by the end of September when the first nuts began to fall to the ground. Armed with a basket, a book, and a mortar and pestle, I got to work.

A single Indian family, I read, collected up to 500 pounds of acorns each fall to last through the winter. The Indians generally stored the nuts whole until they wanted to eat them, and would then process a small portion at a time as needed. I wasn't interested in quantity, at least this first time, and I was eager to taste a finished acorn product. So I gathered, cracked, ground, and leached in one continuous process, day after day after day.

It didn't take long to realize that the books hadn't told me all that I needed to know. When, for example, was the right time to begin gathering the nuts? Was I right to wait until they started to fall to the ground, or would it have been better to shake them from the tree? Answer, from my experience: It is possible to collect them as soon as the nuts are fully formed and have lost their greenish hue. At this point they will fall easily from the tree if the branches are shaken. Acorns on the ground are just as good, though if they've been there in the rain they are likely to have started molding and won't keep well. That fall I collected acorns over a period of a month, both before and after frost, and the freezing temperatures didn't seem to make any difference.

Should I shell them first, then dry them, or vice versa? And how exactly do I shell them? Answer: Dry them first, by spreading them on a tray in the sun or in a very low oven. Then shell them by holding the acorn vertically, cap side up — but with cap removed — on a flat rock, and striking the top sharply with another rock. The blow will crack the shell and then the nut is easily removed.

Do the moldy and wormy nuts have to be sorted out or will the processing render them edible, too? Answer: I let common sense be my guide. A little bit of mold seemed to be fine and I have removed worms by hand with no damage to the nut.

I have since learned that the worms are the larvae of moths who infest the oak, flying around them in the spring and then laying eggs which become worms in the acorn. The Indians controlled the problem by burning the underbrush and the first worm-infested acorns that dropped each fall, so that the moths never took over the tree. The remaining acorns would be shaken from the branches and gathered on the fire-cleared ground below. Without that yearly care, the oak trees have become so overrun that, from the Indians' point of view, the crop is too worm-ridden to bother with.

But I didn't know that then, and I spent day after day picking out the worms and wondering how the Indians had done it efficiently enough to gather a winter's supply. I did learn some tricks: how to tell by the look and especially by the feel of the acorn whether or not there was a nut intact inside. I learned to discard those with holes without bothering to crack them, since inevitably a worm had already eaten most of the nut meat. And if the acorn was lighter than the others, chances were that the nut inside was either decayed or unformed.

Settled against a hill that was taking on the colors of autumn, I collected and sorted the acorns, used stone tools to shell them, and ground the meat into meal bit by bit using the mortar and pestle. Even though I was processing only a small quantity, learning by trial and error and the extra care demanded by the poor quality of the acorns by Indian standards stretched my days into a week and more. But the days were well used. I had time to become familiar with the acorns and the trees they fell from, time to sink into the hillside and feel at home on the earth, now damp from early rain. I had time to sit and watch the trees turn to yellow and brown, and time to wonder if this tree or that had been a favorite of the Indians who used to live here. Slowly, very slowly, working with the acorns changed from a new thing to do to simply the thing that I was doing. Less and less was it an activity; more and more it became life. And one day I realized that perhaps the trees were coming to accept me; I was beginning to feel as if I belonged.

Raw acorns taste bitter because of the tannin that is present in all parts of the oak tree. Tannin is a strong astringent and has many important medicinal uses — the inner bark of the oak makes a good compress for boils and tea from the bark or root helps treat diarrhea — but it is abrasive to the human digestive system and must be leached out of the acorns before they can be eaten. Since the tannin is water soluble, treating the acorns with water removes it. The Indians commonly dug a pit in the earth, lined it with sand and pine boughs, and filled it with shelled and ground acorns. They poured water through the meal until it was dark and no longer bitter.

I tried a number of different methods as they were described in my books. I found that the simplest was the best for me. After I had pounded a quantity of the acorns to a texture of coarse cornmeal, I put it in a cheesecloth bag (a pillowcase works just as well) and secured it overnight in the stream near the yurt. By morning it was completely leached.

I took the bag into the Big House, spread the wet, dark meal on a tray in a low oven until it was dry, then reground it lightly with my mortar and pestle. We had acorn muffins for dinner and acorn bread the next day. The rich, delicious nutty flavor brought with it thoughts of deep, wet forests, of small bands of simple people, of smoke and dreams of long ago.

Learning the names of the oaks and gathering and eating their nuts was more than a pastime. Before long I began to notice subtle changes in my attitude toward the trees I lived among. They began to take on personalities for me and I grew more aware of little things: the color of their bark, their stance on the side of the hill, the health of their leaves. The impact of their presence in my world grew noticeably; more than just appreciating their beauty of form as I had before, now I felt something from the inside, from some center of life within them. As I walked through the woods, I ran my hands over the tree trunks in genuine fondness, and now and then I would catch myself mumbling words of greeting.

As the seasons changed and my time here lengthened, I found other foods growing wild in great plenty. There were wild blackberries in such quantity that I couldn't begin to eat or even can them all; watercress that choked the streams that ran through the meadow; miner's lettuce that grew in huge patches underneath the alders by the White House. In July the manzanita produced tiny reddish berries by the bushel; I collected some to make a delicious fruit-like punch and ground the rest into flour. And in less abundance, depending on the rainfall, there were wild currants, gooseberries, and black raspberries.

Soon after the rains start until well into the following summer, there are green plants growing everywhere on the meadow and in the woods. I wanted to know them all. Unprepared with even the rudiments of botany, I stocked up on books and began to compare the little line drawings with the living plants I came across each day in my walks. Especially at the beginning, it was like hearing a foreign language for the first time and trying to figure out where one sentence ended and the next began. The growing plants presented a jumble of unknown traits to my untrained eye, and they seemed to bear only faint resemblance to the neat drawings in the books.

To my dismay, I found that the books often disagreed among themselves. There were omissions and overlaps, poor reproductions, and confusion caused by local varieties and colloquial names. To help make some sense of it all, I bought a little notebook where I pressed a sample of every plant I found of whose identification I was reasonably certain. Next to the pressed sample I recorded the place found, the date, any peculiar local characteristics, and cross references to its place in my books.

This is how it worked. One afternoon in April I took my pile of books and wandered along the hillside just behind the yurt. I was drawn to a group of delicate little plants with pale blue flowers. Sitting on a nearby log, I reached for one of my books, *The Wild Flowers of California* by Mary Elizabeth Parsons, which was organized by flower color. Let's see, here's the section on blue and purple flowers. Hound's tongue? No; the flower looks similar, but the foliage is way off. Brodeia? No, I know what it looks like. Violet nightshade? No, wrong leaves. Purple nemophilia? Leaves look sort of like it, but the flower's too small. Blue-eyed grass? No. Here! Baby-blue-eyes, waterleaf family. Picture's not just right, but in leafing through the rest of the section, it seems to come the closest to the little plants growing at my feet.

I decide to check my guess in another book. *Wild Edible Plants* by Donald Kirk lists a waterleaf, but not baby-blue-eyes, and the drawing looks nothing like this plant. But *The Leaf Book* by Ida Geary, which has actual leaf prints, include baby-blue-eyes, and the print is a perfect match to this plant. I pick a leaf and a flower for my own file, press it in the notebook and write down identification information. I look back to *Wild Edible Plants* and find that the whole waterleaf family is good in salads; the leaves and roots may also be eaten cooked. I pick a little more for my salad tonight, but am careful to leave enough of the plants so they will continue to grow on this hillside.

In the shade of the log I am sitting on is a flower that looks just like the iris my mother used to plant in her garden, though this plant is much more delicate and the flower itself rests almost on the ground instead of two feet in the air. This is an easy identification: all the books agree that it

[ 118 ]

is a wild iris. Edith van allen Murphy says in *Indian Uses of Native Plants* that a tea from the boiled root is a sure cure for venereal disease. Also, placing the root in a cavity of a tooth is supposed to kill the tooth's nerve, after which the tooth will drop out. Edward K. Balls, in *Early Uses of California Plants,* adds that the Yokia squaws of Mendocino County are said to have wrapped their babies in iris leaves while they were out on the hot dry hillsides collecting manzanita berries. The leaves helped slow the babies' perspiration and saved them from thirst. I marvel at the many purposes the plants served and at a people whose lives were so closely entwined with the lives of the plants they lived among.

Up the hill a little way is a delicate tulip-shaped flower with hairy petals that looks vaguely familiar. Since it has a bluish hue, I wonder if perhaps I just passed it in the Parsons book while I was looking for baby-blue-eyes. I leaf back through the blue and purple section. There it is: in the lily family, its name is cat's ears. I reach out to stroke the little flower, tiny and pert and looking quite like its namesake. *Wild Edible Plants* says that the bulbs are delicious raw or cooked but suggests that since the flower is so beautiful, it should not be picked unless really needed. I decide to forego the sample for my notebook, and instead merely enter date, time, place, and description.

But that is it for the day. The next plant I come across stumps me for nearly half an hour before I give up; likewise the next, and the next, until I realize it is enough.

Funny how it was. Because I learned from books instead of from someone who knew, and because at first I didn't know enough even to tell what family a plant was in, I learned very slowly and erratically. Some days nothing made any sense at all and other days I would turn to the page with the plant's name almost immediately.

[ 119 ]

What happened was that it began to feel as if the plants were in control and teaching me themselves. I wondered if that was what Andy had meant when he said he learned the oaks' names just by living here. Time, my chosen method, and the plants themselves began to interact to teach me more than just the names and uses. I learned to slow down, to calm myself before I went on a plant walk. If I was in a hurry, my eyes wouldn't work right; I couldn't see the patterns of the leaves and flowers. I learned to be polite, to ask the plant its name and character instead of demanding it. A subtle change in attitude, but it seemed to make a difference.

I began to see more, to be able to pick out similarities and family traits. I found plants I had never noticed before in places I had walked by a hundred times; perhaps I hadn't been ready to see them before. The plants, both named and not, took on personalities for me. I began to approach them as friends, as beings with vital essence, partners on the earth. I sat more and walked less. Sometimes I would sit in front of a plant for an hour or more, just watching, before I would open a book. I would notice how the leaves were formed, how the flower settled on the stem, how the insects crawled up and down the leaf, how the petals swayed in the breeze. I learned to be quieter than I had ever been before. Suddenly the world began to seem very full of life and of the miracles that are green plants.

More and more, wild greens became part of my diet. I gathered miner's lettuce, field mint, plantain, shepherd's purse, and chickweed for my salad; I steamed brodeia bulbs, dandelion roots, purslane, watercress, and more mint on top of rice. I could gather enough greens for a simple meal without ranging far from the yurt and it felt very friendly, somehow, to be eating these newfound companions.

I had stopped eating meat several months before we even thought of buying land. I did it then for health reasons, to lose weight and feel

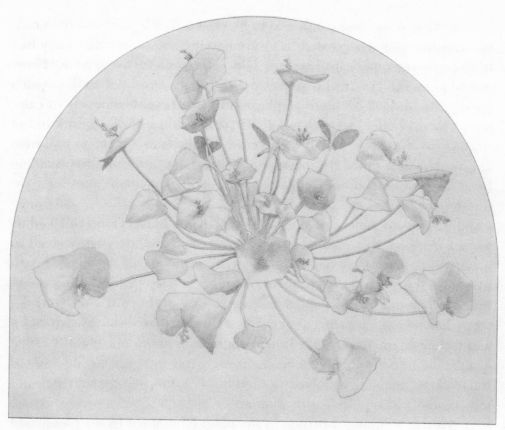

*Miner's Lettuce*

lighter. Most of us have continued to be vegetarians here for more practical reasons — our refrigeration is unpredictable and meat spoils too easily to make it reasonable to keep on hand. But before too long after we moved here, the practical reasons were overshadowed by the ethical ones for me. As we took on more responsibility for the basic elements of our lives — food, shelter, warmth — I felt that I should be willing to kill and prepare an animal if I was going to eat it. Some who wanted to eat meat did undertake the whole process — remember the hunting discussion? — But I decided I could not feel good about taking the life of another creature for my own.

Imagine my shock, then, the afternoon in May of our third year, when I snapped the stem of a miner's lettuce and suddenly felt it dead in my hand. Dead. By my hand. Suddenly all of my newly developed sensitivity to and understanding of plants came out to slap me in the face. Was this why plants had revealed themselves to me? So I could kill them?

I had several moments of genuine anguish when all of my principles and feelings seemed to collide in one big knot in my stomach and I railed against the impossible, cruel choices of life. And then just as suddenly as it had come, the knot dissolved, something fell into place inside me, and the anguish was replaced with wonder.

Without thinking, I turned to the plant lying dead in my hand, and whispered, in the way of the Indian, "O little green plant, I ask that your spirit be added to mine. May I kill always only out of need and with respect. And may I be ever conscious of the Eternal Life that unites all creatures, that makes killing part of living, dying part of rebirth, cycle after cycle, time neverending."

# IX
# One Woman's Liberation

THE FLOW of monthly blood. It moves dark within me, mystery beyond telling. Conception missed, eggs gone free: my uterus — tender, swollen, empty — molts, from the inside out.

The blood flow marks me: I am one with womankind and I am unique. The life force finds its course within and through me. Never do I feel as close to the earth and its rhythms. I retreat, animal-like, in the tradition of Indian women who came before me here. I meditate on the mystery of Woman, thus revealed, but never fully explained or understood.

I had to come to the land to meet myself as woman. My masculine part flourished in the city. But here, on the crest of the meadow, reason has admitted the power of intuition, and creativity has made room for receiving. The earth feeds my moods. I surrender to nature's mysteries and find them reflected in my body, my emotions, my spirit. I walk to the edge of words and step into the pool of knowing.

Sandy is a cowboy from Idaho who has been caretaking the farm five miles down the road for the past three months. He is tall and handsome, with hair the color of his name and a smile that sparkles from somewhere deep within. Having been born and raised on the ranch in Idaho where his parents still live, he knows the woods and its creatures intimately. What is most appealing to me, though, is his fresh and disarming self-confidence, which has somehow remained uncorrupted from a childhood spent on the land despite several years in the city and the armed forces.

Sandy's caretaking stint is a favor to some cousins of his mother. When he returns to Idaho in December he will marry his childhood sweetheart, and they plan to homestead on a piece of his father's ranch. The money Sandy earns by this voluntary exile will help them get started.

In all of his thirty-some years, Sandy has never met folks quite like us, and he has taken to spending the evening here often, sitting around talking and playing his harmonica. Sometimes, if no one is at the Big House, he comes out to the yurt and we talk about bears and mountain lions and how to keep warm in the winter. I am completely charmed by his company and delighted by his stories of the forests he grew up with, which seem remarkably akin to these around here. The differences in our backgrounds hinder no part of our companionship, which often extends late into the night.

One night near the end of his stay, I came back to the yurt after dinner at the Big House. It was cold and dark, with a bit of a drizzle in the air. The dogs went off chasing something as we climbed the last hill and I entered the yurt alone. As soon as I pulled aside the door blanket, I knew something was wrong. The darkness felt strange. I struck a match for the lamp and saw the reason: there was a dim figure stretched out on my bed. I gasped in surprise. It took me a moment to recognize that the figure was Sandy, and even then my heart demanded a number of deep breaths before it would beat normally again.

Sandy roused himself, awakened by the light. "Oh, hi," he said. "I hope I didn't scare you."

"Just nearly to death," I said. "But it's okay. Why didn't you come to the Big House? I didn't hear your car."

"I didn't drive," Sandy said. "I decided to take a walk and just ended up here. Then you weren't here, so I just lay down to wait, and I guess I fell asleep. Sorry," he added again.

"It's okay," I repeated. "Well, how are you anyway? Want some tea?"

He did, but he wanted some company more. He was homesick; his voice and eyes betrayed all the symptoms. The rain started down in earnest, accentuating the little haven of warmth and light that was the yurt. I fixed tea and tried some of the subjects that we had enjoyed talking about before. But tonight nothing caught on. All Sandy wanted was Idaho and his sweetheart. And if she wasn't there, well, I would just have to do. He wanted to spend the night.

Aargh. Well, there it was; I had expected it to come up sooner or later. Why wasn't it as simple as it seemed? Here was one of the nicest human beings I had ever met, to whom I was certainly attracted. Maybe it was that simple for some people. Then why not for me? I didn't have the answer, but I had been a child of the seventies for long enough to know that it wasn't. Somehow I knew that doing what seemed natural and felt good would end up evoking feelings and expectations that had no business being there.

And yet at the same time, I also knew that all of me wasn't in agreement on the subject. Part of me wanted nothing more than to hold him, to transcend our separateness and warm each other on this cold night.

So, well, no, I guess not, I said, feeling about fourteen-and-a-half. Why not? he said. Well, I said, grasping for a reason that might make

[ 125 ]

sense, what about your sweetheart? Oh, yes. Deep down he obviously wanted to be true to her, and I could see the same battle waging in him. Well, I guess you're right, he said, believing it no more than I.

But now that it was finally spoken, all the sexual tension that had been between us for weeks came to the surface. And in true adolescent fashion, we tried to laugh it off, covering up our awkwardness and frustration with hollow banter. I didn't like it and found myself resenting the intrusion of sex into what had been a lovely friendship.

Ah, well, he finally said. Enough. Time to go, right? Right. Tired as we both were, of the day and of the conversation, it was definitely time to go.

He put on his shoes and got his jacket and hat. Then he looked at me with a particular caution in those gentle brown eyes, as if something had just occurred to him. "Now don't worry," he said. And he reached under the bed and pulled out a holster and gun.

My heart stopped for the second time that night, and this time it seemed to suspend entirely. It took me several very long moments of staring at the gun to come to my senses and realize that of course he wasn't going to shoot me. My heart started again, racing, and I giggled weakly.

"I always carry a gun when I'm in the woods," he explained, seeing how it looked to me. "Done it ever since I was a kid. Never can tell when you'll need it, you know." He laughed a little nervously, then turned and went into the night.

I laugh at it now, and tell the story as another good joke on me, city kid that I am, unaccustomed to the ways of the real old-timers in the woods. But at the time, the fear evoked by the sight of that gun in the hands of a man I had just sent away was very real, even if it passed quickly. I can attribute that reaction, in part at least, to shell shock from the ranch version of the war between the sexes, a partial personal account of which follows. But there is more. I also reacted to the latent violence of the moment, the very real violence that seems to be the darker side of sex. And from that perspective, my perception was a true one, despite its lack of correlation with Sandy's intentions.

The story that follows is drawn from the same level of awareness. It is a journey of mind and psyche, not objective fact. And it is a journey of only one woman's psyche. Most of the men and many of the women who have experienced these same events would recount them differently.

But it is true nevertheless. This is really how it was for me. To say that what follows was a product of my own mind merely sets the stage upon which the whole struggle seems to transpire, and from which it occasionally threatens to spill over into whatever we choose to call "objective reality."

When we moved to the ranch, sexism was a political issue for me, but I didn't see its relevance to my own life. I was a single woman, successful, competent, "liberated," and I felt no particular scars or restrictions from a sexist society. My parents had raised me to feel I could do whatever I wanted in life, and I had never run up against anything in the world outside that contradicted that feeling. I had lived in houses with men before, and had worked closely with them, but I had never experienced the deep and long-term intimacy that living together at the ranch instilled. Here, where mundane details had the power to touch my secret self and its unspoken dreams, my simplistic dismissal of women's causes met its inevitable challenge.

The first and most obvious issue was work roles. By the middle of the first summer, most of the women were working long days in the garden, along with the men, and still carrying the major burden of cooking the big evening meal. We all agreed to institute a schedule to adjust this disparity: one man and one woman would be in charge of cooking and cleaning each day. The schedule — to which we all turned out to be allergic — lasted only a month, but the incident gave us a good chance to add sexism to the growing list of issues to discuss at those first summer meetings.

By the first fall, with spirits bruised and egos battered from the rhetoric of those discussions, most of us retreated to pick up the pieces. But somewhere inside me a deeper connection had been made: I no longer saw women's liberation as a cause only for all the other women in the world; I was excited about the possibilities of applying it in my own life. I began to analyze our interactions with attention to social conditioning and to read "women's writers," such as Shulamith Firestone and Elizabeth Gould. And I shared knowing looks with Carol when something particularly "sexist" happened.

For most of that winter and into the next spring, my thoughts continued to center on work roles and the inequalities they perpetuated. Sometime in the winter, Bruce countered the standard feminist arguments by objecting to the control the women exerted over the kitchen. He said he felt continually put down by women in the areas of traditional female domination, child care and cooking, even though he liked to do both of those things. And Michael went on to point out that sharing work roles went both ways: until then the men had been carrying almost the entire burden of plumbing, cutting firewood, and mechanical work.

Over the next several months, most of us made an effort to rectify those areas of imbalance. Carol learned to accommodate Bruce in the kitchen, and many of the women set to work at acquiring the skills to fix the water pipes and clean a carburetor. During that spring I realized that most of the ranch work was by then divided along lines of personality rather than sex. Ranger had developed a variety of culinary specialties, including egg drop soup and French bread; Russell was nearly a fixture at the sink washing dishes; Susie helped with a major repair of the Big House plumbing; and Carol was becoming an expert with the chain saw. The same was true for decision making: power was held more by the force of personality than of gender, and even then it was subject to the quirks of the issue at hand.

But for some reason, realizing that we had few further problems with work-role oppression or lack of access to decision-making power didn't satisfy my growing feminist sensitivities. I still felt a basic disharmony between men and women, and the issue of work roles now seemed almost insignificant by comparison. My reading turned to psychology, and I eagerly began studying my relationships from an elementary (and self-serving) understanding of male and female principles.

Here is an excerpt from my journal at the time:

"It seems to me that the differences between the sexes are very deep, deeper than the cultural trappings, and antagonized by them. The crucial differences for me are the differences in the ways men and women feel about commitment, responsibility, love. I find it hard to understand, accept, or live with the male versions of those things."

Once I realized that men and women were such radically different creatures, the fact seemed to be confirmed by nearly every interaction I had or observed. The fundamental difference explained the gnawing uneasiness I had occasionally noticed with men before. It also evoked two other, more powerful emotions. On the one hand, I felt deeply betrayed by the discovery that half the human race didn't think or, more important, *feel*, as I did. And on the other hand, I was deeply excited by the

[ 129 ]

sense of a vital level of personal meaning that seemed to lie waiting for me beneath the surface of sexual differences.

Strangely, perhaps, both of those emotions fueled my anger, which had been self-righteously sparked way back when we were dealing with work-role problems. The feeling of betrayal is an obvious enough road to anger. But the sense of potential fulfillment proved effective fuel too. For a time, understanding the dynamics of the male-female principles seemed to promise the answer to all the mysteries of life, and I therefore adopted a feminist filter through which I routed all my perceptions. Developing my feminist consciousness, as I phrased it, became my primary growth priority and brought with it some unpleasant side effects.

Again from my journal: "The more aware I become, the less tolerance I have for anyone who doesn't seem to be making an effort to shake off that cultural male-female conditioning. I want it to be right, NOW. I don't want to wait. My emerging feminist consciousness is the most important thing in my life now, and I am impatient with anyone who doesn't share that priority. . . . I am uncovering a lot of anger in me, toward the culture I grew up in, toward men in general and toward the men I live with. I know that hasn't been easy on them. It isn't easy for me either. Sometimes I dream of living with only women."

The politics of feminism had, up to now, split the ranch women along lines of personality and style. Susie and Annie were turned off by the rhetoric, just as Carol and I thrived on it. We women had never really united behind an issue. But now, as I became increasingly frustrated with men, I sought the comforting sameness and support of other women more and more. One month when we all ran out of Tampax at the same time, I realized our menstrual cycles were coordinated. It was a tangible manifestation of our connections.

We did talk about having a men's house and a women's house, but nothing ever came of it. I began to begrudge the predominance of the "male" style of relationship (characterized by noise, jest, and food fights) in our communal functions, and to resent daily interactions with people who did not see things the way I did.

And then, into that mire of hypersensitivity and self-righteousness, in the summer of 1973, came summer camp.

In fact this was the second summer we had a camp. In 1972, Susie and Michael organized a two-week camp for ten children, with gratifying success. This summer we planned a larger and longer-termed effort: thirty children, aged eight to fourteen, for six weeks. We advertised in the Bay Area, made some arrangements with inner-city agencies to sign up their kids, and tried to interview as many prospective campers as possible ahead of time. We were aware that we might have some problems: a number of the children came from unhappy homes, and some had potentially violent behavior patterns. But our faith in the healing, wholesome effects of the country was boundless. I made lists of camp songs from my own glorious childhood experience and anticipated evenings of meaningful talk round the campfire, days working together in the garden or learning about wild plants.

The explosion that accompanied the children's first meeting with one another on the hot, dry, dusty meadow did away with all those flowery fantasies in short order. The "campers" could have cared less about gardening or even swimming (if they had to walk a mile to get there); all they seemed to want to do was jive and bully each other and us. Every group activity we were able to motivate was incidental to the overwhelming struggle with violence that was going on at every level. It became the on-going theme and continuity of the summer.

I wasn't prepared for being a target of that anger. I remembered idolizing my camp counselors, and naturally I expected similar relation-ships with these children. But most of these kids had been sent here with-out their cooperation, and so quite naturally they came already thinking of us as their jailers. That feeling was heightened for many of them: the country, with its wide open spaces and foreign creatures and sounds, was a de facto jail — and it scared them to death.

I had decided to live outdoors with a group of the older children in a clearing behind the yurt. The idea was for all of us to build a large lean-to out of natural materials and cook two meals a day over an open fire. As it turned out, the older children were all boys — seven of them between the ages of eleven and fourteen. Bruce and Ranger agreed to help out, and I saw no reason not to go ahead with my plans, not even when all but two of the group declared that it was the dumbest idea they'd ever heard.

I pretended not to hear, and with forced enthusiasm I led them off toward the Lean-To Village site. We had dinner with the rest of the camp that evening, but I had planned roasted marshmallows and a campfire later to get our little group off to a cozy start. I had figured we could talk about the lean-to we would build and plan some other exciting things to do together.

It didn't quite work out that way. Roasting marshmallows started out with J. B. worrying that someone might be getting more than he was, progressed to some not-so-friendly efforts at making everyone else's marsh-mallow but one's own fall into the fire, and ended in a decidedly hostile battle with hot, sticky, and sharp marshmallow sticks. I resorted to au-thoritarianism and declared it was time for bed.

The next morning I discovered that not one of them had understood that I had suggested building one large lean-to for all of us. The thought simply hadn't registered. Before I had the breakfast fire going, each one of them was out looking for a place for his own — and certainly superior — house. I thought that was a striking example of selective hearing but decided not to interfere. Maybe trying to outbuild each other was the best way for them to discover some enthusiasm.

The power struggle took shape immediately. Though there were temporary shifts of affiliation as the summer progressed, in general it was Don, J. B., and Eddie against Danny and Joel. Billy aligned himself with whoever seemed to be on top at any particular moment, and Enoch was pretty much against everyone all the time. Don spent many creative hours devising suitable names to call Danny, concentrating on those which would say something about Danny's mental capacity (which in fact was clearly superior). Billy entertained whoever would listen with an endless series of dirty stories. Enoch announced one evening that he was going to kill Joel the next morning. He got his handsome black face right up close to Joel's and said, "Boy, you're dead." Joel didn't waste time arguing, but decided to sleep at the White House that night. Halfway through the six weeks, Eddie was helping me cut something up for dinner when he paused to contemplate the twelve-inch-long kitchen blade he was using. "This is the same kind of knife that I tried to kill myself with," he said.

Elsewhere on the ranch things were similarly difficult. The four streetwise inner-city kids pretty much terrorized the others, mostly with bluff and jive, but laced with real muscle when required for credibility. The day that they organized the rest of the older kids to disrupt the treasure hunt that Carol had carefully planned for the younger ones, Michael loaded all the older boys into the truck and dumped them ten miles down the road. By the time they got back, they were so angry that they tore the steps off the second-story porch of the White House in retaliation.

To be fair, I have to admit that the picture I've drawn is something of a caricature. There were some moments of genuine friendship, and several of the adults and children seemed to be having a pretty good time. Not everyone shudders when thinking about this summer. But I do. For me the caricature was a depressing reality. I struggled through the summer with great difficulty only because I was genuinely fond of some of the children (difficulties notwithstanding) and because there was really no choice.

So camp continued. Somehow we managed to adapt our grandiose plans to the situation before us, and the children went swimming, learned how to weave baskets, and ate three meals a day. The recurrent fact of those three meals made us realize very quickly why most summer camps hire cooks and kitchen staff; finding time and energy for food planning, preparation, and clean-up often seemed one thing too many. And yet, of course, meals had to come first, as centuries of mothers have known.

Instinctively, we women turned to each other for help and support in that work. We knew without having to discuss it that whatever our differences about a woman's role in the kitchen may have been, this was a high-pressure situation and we would rely on each other to do what needed to be done. I knew Debby would put away the cheese after lunch if I left it out by mistake, and Carol knew I would start the beans soaking for dinner if she forgot. But even more important than preparing the food was the presence of feminine intuition and caring that the food symbolized. I knew that Annie would perceive the needs of a troubled camper as I did, and that she — and Susie and Deb and Carol and Kathy — would all be sensitive to what they could do to help. Perhaps because of the particular situation and personalities, perhaps because of the point I had reached in my male-female analysis before camp began, I did not trust the men to see or do any of those things or even to care whether they were done or not. The pressure of the time magnified my distrust and seemed to create one situation after another in which my expectations were borne out. There probably were other exceptions like Ranger's egg drop soup for forty, but they didn't register in my increasingly critical mind.

A dream I had then is particularly revealing. My parents are coming to visit the ranch for the first time, and I am desperately trying to clean up in preparation. Susie and Carol are helping. Time is running out, and I am getting more and more nervous. Susie and Carol share my anxiety and are working as frantically as I am. Suddenly Ashley walks in the door of the White House, onto the kitchen floor which we have just finished scrubbing, and dumps a bucket of water over my head, in jest. Furious, I grab him by his nose and throw him out of the house through the window.

The dream shows clearly how I felt: not only did men not understand what was important to women, not only did they not take it seriously, but they went even further and tromped all over and messed up things that were special and meaningful to women. That male-female interaction feels deeply accurate to me still. In the dream I reacted to the difference in values with anger, throwing Ashley out of the house by his nose, an appendage which bears psychological resemblance to another long, protruding male body part. In "real life" I reacted in classical female fashion: I turned into a shrew. I recognized centuries of women in myself and hated the woman I had become as much as I felt helpless to be otherwise. I was amazed at the almost instinctive force of my shrewing; it was as if, animal-like, I had evolved a new form for survival. The shrewing was a way of covering up a deep hurt, a defensive posture against a male world that ignored, scorned, and laughed at some of my deepest female impulses.

By the end of summer camp I was aching for a little tenderness. Six weeks of "I can do it better than you can" and "Joel is so stupid" had left me shaken and fragile. Everything I had thought and read in the preceding few years about society's pressures on little girls and boys paled before the astonishing evidence of how it *felt* to be a prepuberty little boy in America.

I said goodbye to the children almost mechanically and turned to the task of cleaning up and getting life back to normal. I was exhausted emotionally and spiritually. The escalating pressure of the summer had turned the anger that had simmered within me for the past couple of years into all-out war in my psyche. And I had not liked the results. My personal metamorphosis from reasonable, sweet human being into irritable shrew left me astonished and depressed. Further, I could see that my reaction had made the general male-female climate worse instead of better. Justified or not, generally anger had brought forth a response in kind; the hostility between men and women seemed to have encouraged us to build even thicker the walls that prevented our mutual understanding.

And I didn't like the way I felt inside. What had happened to that promise of a new meaning that seemed so close some months before? Now I wanted nothing so much as to retreat into a peaceful sexless existence. Anger had had its place in the growing of my consciousness; it had helped me to define myself and reclaim control over my life. But now I saw that the noise and self-righteousness of my anger had obscured what liberation was all about.

Why had the struggle evoked so much energy from me anyway? What *was* it all about?

It wasn't until several months after the close of summer camp that I realized that I had undergone an imperceptible but significant change of emphasis, from without to within. The outer struggle, I saw then, had nearly caught me in a trap of its own: trying to be a better, more efficient man than men were. But somewhere in the heat of the battle of summer camp, despite or perhaps because of the turmoil it inspired in me, I had experienced something of the transforming power of deep, and apparently uniquely female, instincts.

That felt good, exciting and redeeming, an affirmative avenue of growth. But even that was not the end, not the promise that had caused me to turn my life around in its pursuit. The promise was Liberation, which is but another way of saying Truth or God, and the male-female struggle was only one aspect of that larger quest. It was an important aspect, to be sure — an effort to bring my dark parts into light, to understand the conflicting desires and impulses that are within me, and to fulfill the potential that is uniquely me. But important only in service of the larger goal — and there, I finally understood one spring day many months after summer camp, was where I'd gone astray.

I had been stockpiling those hard-won understandings of myself and others as weapons of war to use in "winning" the battle between the sexes. In consequence, the struggle, which had seemed to promise so much, degenerated into a bitter clash of ego. But I saw now that the real value of my newfound insights was precisely to give me a choice I hadn't had before — to move beyond the battle. The light of understanding offered me the option of release from the blind compulsion of semiconscious feelings; I could, if I chose, use that understanding not to wound but rather to take me where I really wanted to go. I could ask that understanding to serve my true goal, which was not victory over the male half of the race, but personal liberation.

What sweet relief. I felt the bitterness and confusion of the previous months subside within. I saw, finally and certainly, that the promise of the male-female struggle would be fulfilled only when that lesser effort was dedicated to the search that lies beyond all superficial distinctions, the search for God. And in the peace of that realization, the promise glowed as bright and firm as ever: to understand, in order to be truly, absolutely, and forevermore, free.

# X
# Not a School, Exactly

WHEN WE came here, my feelings about education were the product of some combination of pleasant memories of being a student, a frustrating but enlightening teaching experience at Rivendell, and a gut-level conviction that in most schools the accent was in the wrong place. I felt that education should be active instead of passive, books needed to be combined with experience to make sense, and the whole process must be voluntary in order to work.

My view at that time was that learning was the central purpose of life, the source of all human progress and the potential answer to all human dilemmas. I still feel that way, though time has altered what I mean when I use most of those words.

Almost immediately I realized that the ranch was the most stimulating environment I had ever been in — intellectually, emotionally, physically, and spiritually. Each day brought new excitement and new challenges, and I felt myself stretch as never before to learn and to use and integrate my learning. Not in my most memorable college classes had everything meshed and inspired me quite this way.

That feeling lasted past the initial adjustment and continued to grow, so that by the time we were ready to open the full-time school that had been our original incentive for this whole venture, I was looking forward to the chance to introduce young people to this environment, in the expectation that they would discover the same stimulation here that I had.

By that time, the fall of 1974, we were a licensed foster home, and three of the eight teenagers who joined us were our foster children, placed here through a San Francisco agency — Doug, 17; Bill, 16, who became Cougar midway through the school year; and Tammy, 12. Jan, 18, who had taken two years out of school and therefore did not yet have her high school diploma, also found out about us through an agency in the city. Selora, 14, and Nick, 12, had been here to summer camp. Camper, 12, and Hawk, 16, came through personal contacts with their parents. Including Kristine and Josie, who were 8 and 6 at that time, and, less regularly, T. A., who was 4, we had eleven students.

We gave Jan and Selora the Stream House, converted the White House into a dormitory with rotating resident adult for Tammy, Camper, and Nick, and Doug, Cougar, and Hawk moved back and forth between the Big House and various structures of their own devising.

We adults drew up a list of classes we'd like to teach, which ranged from geography with Ash and Michael to piano with Carol to a study of the California Indians with Bruce and me. The subjects were about evenly distributed between hard-core academics like remedial reading by Susie and "fun" classes like drama by James, who had joined the ranch family the year before. Most tried to combine learning and doing, such as "people's technology" by Bruce and Michael, which taught basic principles of math and physics through actual work projects. In addition to the regular classes, we suggested that each student choose one area for in-depth independent study under the guidance of one of us.

We circulated the list of proposed classes to the students as soon as they arrived, and asked for their suggestions of other things they'd like to learn. After three days of settling in and getting to know each other, we started the first day of real "school" by gathering at the head of the meadow to match up areas of interest and devise a schedule.

Deborah cooked an early breakfast at the Big House. She and Bruce had found the season's first chicken mushroom in the woods the day before. Chicken mushrooms are a wild, rubbery, edible fungus that grows on oak trees. The year before we had found that a fried slice of the strange yellow thing tastes a lot like chicken — especially if your eyes are closed. Chicken mushroom omelettes seemed a perfect way to initiate the students into the ways of living in the country, close to the abundance of nature. Everyone was hungry, energy was high, and Deborah cooked a lot of rich, delicious breakfasts.

Stomachs full, we adjourned to the meadow. It was the first week in October and the weather was spectacular. Cool, fresh air flowed easily over the meadow; on the distant hills the poison oak showed red, and we could see touches of yellow where the maples were beginning to turn. We arranged ourselves around the fallen log at the top of the meadow, just below the curve of the driveway. Susie took out her notebook and pencil. We went around the circle and the students outlined the courses of study they had chosen. Jan: math, Indians, and independent dream study with Bruce. Cougar: work on high school equivalency. Camper: reading, math, and drama. Tammy: where was Tammy? Someone had seen her go into the White House. Nick went to check. They came back together, Tammy pale and grinning faintly, embarrassed to admit that she had just been very sick. Strange.

We continued. Tammy: people's technology — "Does that mean

science?" she asked — drama, and art. Selora: weaving, Indians, and math. Kristine: reading and writing, math, horseback riding, stained glass.

Doug: uh-oh, Doug had disappeared, too. And there was Nick heading toward the White House. Suddenly Susie turned pale, put down pencil and notebook, and excused herself. The White House bathroom was more than full. In no mood to wait, we took to the hills, one by one. And then returned, only a little green, to laugh at the next victim. The school year had officially opened.

*Note:* The cause of our sudden sickness remains a mystery. The closest we could come to an explanation was that this particular fungus had been growing on the inside of a hollow tree rather than on a fallen log that was exposed to light and circulating air. Perhaps its location contributed to an excess of tannin, the same astringent found in acorns that upsets the digestive system. All the chicken mushrooms we had eaten the year before had come from fallen logs, and brought no ill effects.

In our planning for the school, we rejected any trace of an authoritarian structure — including any distinctions, verbal or otherwise, between "students" and "adults" (a practice I have not followed in this chapter, in the interests of clarity) — in the confidence that learning would be a natural and enjoyable part of living together. But it was quickly obvious that it would be a while before the "learning is a natural part of living" principle led to Socratic dialogues or even to enthusiastic ecological study. "Living," for many of these kids, had already been turbulent and confusing beyond their years. Living, for them, meant surviving; and learning, first off, meant accumulating and developing the tools of that trade.

No one made higher grades in that endeavor than Tammy, Nick, and Camper. By the end of the first week of school, they had solidified into a guerilla unit dedicated to heading off adult intervention in their lives. Their repertoire included an imaginative array of diversionary tactics and psychological warfare. But my full initiation didn't come until it was my turn to be White House houseparent during the two weeks before Christmas break.

Up until then, since they weren't in any of my classes, my only contacts with Tammy, Nick, and Camper had been at dinner and meetings. Their almost incessant teeny-bopper jive was tedious, but a taste of fresh twelve-year-old poked through the hip facade often enough that I knew I was going to like getting to know them better.

So I was looking forward to spending some relaxed time together by sharing living quarters for a while. My first night as houseparent, I left the Big House while everyone else was still lingering over Carol's spice cake so I could have the White House feeling like home by the time the kids arrived. I lit the lamps, stoked up the fire, and straightened things in the living room. By the time I heard Tammy, Camper, and Nick laughing and shouting their way down the driveway, I was snuggled into the big red chair, feet up away from the drafty floor, reading.

Clomp, clomp. Sound of boots on linoleum.

"Hey, it's Barb!"

"Hi, Mom!"

"You our mom now?"

"You gonna fix us nighttime treats?" (As a matter of fact, the milk was already heating for hot chocolate.)

"Hey, have you seen our cubbies?"

They take me up to the loft. Their cubbies are secret hideouts, fashioned ingeniously from odd corners of their rooms. They each have one, barely big enough to contain the four of us. Secret stashes, secret places. I am dimly aware of being conned into complicity with the honor of receiving pseudoprivileged information. "Now here's where we keep our stash." Tammy pulls out a half empty bottle of peach brandy. "Now you can't tell anyone, see?"

"And you can't come up without asking," Camper adds.

"When we're here, it's private, see?" Nick contributes. And as an afterthought, "Hey, are you one of those that's going to be talking about cleaning up all the time?"

I remember the milk heating, and go down to mix the cocoa. Do they want popcorn, too? "Sure!" Tammy yells back.

"Hey, Barb, you're all right!" Camper pronounces loudly.

Nick shouts down, "You can just put it on the dumbwaiter when it's ready."

Dumbwaiter? An orange crate, they show me, that they have rigged up so that they can raise and lower it by rope through a pulley bolted to a roof beam. Clever way to avoid going up and down the ladder with full hands or, perhaps more to the point, to avoid any more contact than necessary with the adults who prowl the downstairs.

I put the popcorn on, keep the cocoa hot. From above my head I hear Nick turn on his battery-operated radio. KFRC, San Francisco. Footsteps head toward Camper's cubby. Low voices, shuffle of cards. Then the radio is turned up, drowning out any other noise.

When the popcorn is ready, I put it and the cocoa (in a closed jar) on the dumbwaiter and watch it slowly rise into the darkness.

"Thanks, Mom!"

"Hey, Barb, you're all right!"

I check the fire, go back to the red chair, put my feet up away from the draft, and reopen my book to the strains of a Golden Oldie. Vaguely I wonder if I was like that at age twelve, and remember that I was. I suspect that the next two weeks will demand that I remember often.

Jan and Selora are lovely, deep, and bright. Selora is tall and slender, with hair long enough to sit on; she is a dancer and an artist, whose sensitive, gracious company is always welcome. Jan's beauty is the kind that makes people on the street stop and stare. She asked me to be her counselor her first week here, and my respect for her intelligence and strength of mind has grown rapidly as I've watched her function on the ranch and our friendship has deepened.

Jan and Selora have been studying California Indians with Bruce and me since September. In the fall we concentrated on learning about food gathering, including a few weeks of collecting and processing acorns. At the beginning of December we began reading about the spiritual quality of Indian life, particularly the Indians' relationship to the natural world. Last week we built a campfire outside in the drizzle and talked about how it must have felt to be an Indian living so closely with nature, and compared our own lives to what we had read. We sat together on the cold, damp ground, in silence, thinking. Then Selora said, "I want to see if I can do it. Let's go someplace like the Indians did, without food, and sleep on the ground."

And so, tonight, we are going to Suicide Rock, a huge flat-topped rock which overlooks the river canyon about four hours' hike from the ranch. In the summer, we get there by walking along the river bed and through the river; now, with the river at full winter height, we will have to pick our way through the forest and along the rocks. It is the February full moon, and we are blessed with a clear, cool night. We plan to leave at moon rise, get to the rock about midnight, then curl around a fire together until dawn.

As I wait for the others at the yurt, I brew a pot of tea. Just as the moon peeks over the horizon, I hear footsteps, and Selora, Jan, and Bruce pull aside my door flap and come in. I pour us each a cup of tea to celebrate the journey ahead. As we drink, mostly in silence, the yurt seems warm and cozy, the night big and cold. I catch Selora's eyes and see the same mixture of excitement and apprehension that I feel. Jan takes a deep breath, hands me her empty cup, and we all giggle a little at nothing in particular. Bruce blows out the lamps, and we head together out into the night.

Down the familiar path to the river, I am transfixed by the changes the moon has wrought on the meadow. What was green and gray by day is now all shades of blue and silver. The moonlight makes distances seem near and flattens the dips and curves of the hills into two dimensions. We walk single file, hardly speaking.

The night is so still that it is almost a surprise to find the river moving. Yet the water rushes ahead undaunted, its roar undiminished by the hush of darkness. The water is thick, deep gray, and cold. We turn up the canyon against the direction of the current, with Bruce in the lead.

About a mile upstream from our present location, the riverbank becomes sheer, startling cliffs. In order to avoid getting caught there and trying to scale unfamiliar slippery rock in the moonlight, Bruce suggests that we veer inland, following a narrow deer path. As we enter the forest, the trees block out the moonlight, except for occasional patches. It seems colder; we step up the pace.

We climb up and away from the river for maybe a half hour until we can no longer hear it and are lost in a forest world. Then we leave the path and head off cross country, parallel to where we guess the river is. Cross-country walking here is difficult in the daylight, with the maze of bush, fallen trees, thick underbrush, and the continuous rise and fall of the earth's surface. The night adds an even greater challenge. The moon makes strange creatures of the forest dwellers: gnarled manzanita limbs reach out like grasping tentacles, a fallen fir log seems to shiver as we pass. The shadows play tricks. Branches appear to be moving, swaying, grabbing at us; the earth itself seems to undulate with a slightly ominous rise and fall. I fancy I can hear breathing under my feet.

Then we are out of the forest, briefly, into a wide and steep meadow. We sit for a moment to rest, glad to be free of the shadows. All four of us stretch out in the moonlight. Far below, the river is visible again, and its sounds rise to meet us. The meadow is so steep that I feel as though I have to pay attention to keep from sliding off.

The meadow leads us to forest again. We pick our way through, between, over, and under twisted branches, tangled roots, fallen limbs. I hear Jan breathing heavily behind me; I notice that Bruce is stumbling; I, too, am having a hard time getting my body to do what I want it to. Selora says her legs are beginning to ache. We continue, down the hill across a creekbed, full of winter waters: we balance on a rock and then on a fallen limb, and make it across with no wet feet. Up the steep hill on the other side, out into an open meadow again.

And there, suddenly, looms Suicide Rock. Much closer than we had thought, much larger than we expected. We are high above the river, but the rock is higher yet, way up there somewhere near the stars. To get to it we are going to have to go all the way down to the river's edge to cross another creek, and up, up the long meadow to its surface.

We run downhill faster than I would have thought possible without benefit of daylight, inspired by a sudden burst of energy at the sight of the rock. We leap across the creek, a bigger one this time. Well, almost across: we come away with three wet feet. The rock seems to grow as we begin the final climb.

Pulling ourselves up the long, steep meadow requires all our remaining energy: up, up, and still up. We pause to rest; we watch the river growing smaller below us, and watch the rock getting closer. A deer trail, with us on it, climbs steeply to the left shoulder of the rock. Then, finally, we are level with its surface. We wind our way through a grove of manzanita, picking up firewood as we go, and then the earth drops away in front of us.

We are at the very edge of the rock, apparently on the crest of the world. The river, 500 feet below, winds sparkling through the canyon, dappled by moonshadow. The stars hum close overhead. The mountains, snow-covered peaks, seem just out of reach. We make a small fire and ease our tired bodies to the earth. We sit, we watch, we listen. A single owl calls, the river flows. We talk a bit. Then one by one, we find our places, and curl up in such a way as to expose maximum body area to the warmth of the fire. There is more wood at arm's length; when the fire begins to die, one of us will stir and feed it again.

I don't sleep much. Curling up on cold, wet ground and sleeping must be a learned art. But I don't really care. Sleeping would mean I might miss something.

Dawn comes early. We rise, stretch aching muscles, and run leaping, bounding, and howling down the meadow and on toward home.

We have been talking about building a mechanics shed for months. Everyone who has worked on cars here has done it out of need rather than choice, and there has never been anyone who had enough pure love for the art to be the force behind setting up a proper work area. So repairs are done under the most impossible of conditions: in the freezing cold, groveling in the mud, with rain pelting down and running around the small of one's back. Fingers stick to cold metal tools, bodies shiver, and tempers shorten in geometric proportion. No wonder we often settle for short-term repairs instead of doing it the long but right way the first time.

So when Doug announces an interest in mechanics our eyes light up. Almost eighteen and a budding counter-culture mad scientist, he inspires renewed interest in building a real mechanics shed that might make working on cars a reasonable pastime. Nothing fancy, just a work surface that is off the ground, sheltered from the rain, with possible future water and electrical hook-ups. Ashley agrees to donate the lumber, and Michael, Mark, and Cougar are willing to contribute labor. All we have to do is find a place to put it.

We have 670 acres to choose from. Well, not exactly. The meadows are off limits and no one wants it very close to his or her house. It needs to be a relatively level place with year-round road access, good winter drainage, available water, preferably located so that sound — thinking of a future generator — won't carry, and somewhat hidden from view.

Doug suggests an old logging landing that is level, near two streams, and clear of brush. Objection: it's along the road to Ashley's house; he'd have to walk by the old car bodies every day.

We look further.

Bruce suggests the old sawmill site. Objection: it's visible from the road, not a safe place to leave tools.

Time passes.

Well, how about up the hill from the sawmill, toward the cabin? No, that's a lovely site for someone's future house, and besides, then Carol would have to walk past old car bodies every day.

More time passes.

Pole City site is too far away from the main houses to make sense. Michael finds a place along the road to Deb and Annie's old campsite: level, but a little nearer the Stream House than Jan and Selora would like, a little nearer the road than James likes. It's beginning to be hard to work up enthusiasm.

Still more time passes. It's been a couple months since we started seriously looking for sites.

Doug finally blows up. Government funds for his support as a foster child run out on his rapidly approaching eighteenth birthday. His time here is drawing to a close, and he's accomplished almost nothing tangible; he has no skill that will help him pay his way when he hits the world on his own. What kind of school is this anyway? Where are our priorities? Why is it so hard to *do* anything?

Good questions. On the defensive, Michael points out that it isn't impossible to do things around here, it just takes some time to figure out the right combination of contemplation, planning, and action, and in any case, the process itself is as important as the result. On the counterattack, Bruce charges that if Doug had shown more dedication and ability to assume responsibility, the shed would have been underway by now. Anything that anyone *really* wants to do here gets done, as long as it is right for the ranch and for the land.

But wait a minute. Maybe that is true from the standpoint of a long-term resident of the ranch, but what importance do things like group process or even care of the land have for someone like Doug, who is here only nine months and then wants to move on to making his own way in the world?

One large part of the problem seems to be that the values of a lifetime rancher and a nine-month student are frequently at odds. This realization forces to the surface a suspicion that has been gently nagging at me for some weeks: the ranch isn't the ideal place of learning for everyone that it is for me. For Jan and for Cougar and maybe for Hawk, the year at the ranch has been close to ideal, for many of the same reasons it is for me: nearly unlimited freedom, time and space to know oneself, stimulation on many levels, the opportunity and necessity to take charge of one's own life. For Doug, those benefits have almost disappeared in his overwhelming need for a marketable skill, which the ranch has not been able to provide. The other students fall somewhere between those extremes; for most of them the year has been well spent, but Selora and Nick are already planning more structured situations for the following September.

By this time, mid-April, another realization is beginning to dawn on me, equally startling for my image of myself and my relationship to the world. I realize that I'm not really a very good teacher. I am finding it increasingly tedious to go over and over material I know by heart with a student who is learning it for the first time. And I lack another quality that is vital in the nonstructure of the ranch school — I seem unable to arouse enthusiasm in others about a topic whose vitality and interest they haven't yet discovered for themselves.

I have just started to write, and I am finding that writing offers an excitement and a positive avenue of connecting with the world that seems more compatible with me than teaching. Writing suddenly seems a truer and more interesting way for me to do the things I had at one time hoped to do by starting a school.

At the same time, the school has developed difficulties of a more practical nature. Tuition doesn't bring in enough money to meet ranch needs, which creates both mental and financial strain. We're faced with the prospect of raising tuition beyond the reach of many of the current students if we are to keep going.

But do we want another year of school? Not everyone has been making the same discoveries about themselves that I have, but I'm not alone in my misgivings about the school. In the years since we have come to the ranch, thinking of ourselves as teachers, many of us have developed new vocational interests and want the time to pursue them. Russell wants to try freelance photography, Carol to grow trees, Susie to do professional counseling. A school as our principal activity no longer seems right.

These discussions, sparked by Doug, continue with some intensity and in various forms for the last two months of the school year. By June I feel that we have all learned something. Each of the students has a pretty clear understanding of his or her intellectual, emotional, and social progress over the previous nine months, and most of them also have a set of personal priorities that is clearer than ever before. Jan and Hawk are ready to take their high school equivalency tests; Selora has learned to weave; Tammy has discovered interest and talent in writing and drawing. Camper has avoided Susie's remedial reading class with great personal delight. Doug has learned to organize public opinion, and Tammy, Nick, and Cougar now know how to express themselves effectively in front of a group. Perhaps most important, each one of the students has a new sense of self-confidence that seems to be a direct result of his or her school year here. I find, somewhat to my surprise, that they all seem a lot older and smarter than they did in September.

We adults, too, are older and smarter. Or at least older. After nine months of round-the-clock, seven-day-a-week availability, we are ready for a break. We have each gone through some personal soul-searching, and the ranch has experienced a major redefinition. We have done the school we came here to do and found that it is not enough to meet our needs, either financial or personal. It is clear to most of us that we want to continue including young people in our lives, but on a reduced scale. We overhaul the ranch finances to establish a monthly fee for each resident adult and begin to make the individual adjustments that the new system will demand.

The last day of school comes, at last. Camper returns to his parents in Maryland, Selora and Tammy get ready for public school in the fall, Mark helps Doug find a job in the city renovating old houses. Jan, Cougar, and Hawk will be with us through the summer and most of next year. The season changes, the faces turn, and life — which is, after all, the most exacting school — continues.

# XI
# The Many and the One

LATE MARCH gives way to April, and April turns toward May. The meadow is ablaze with color. It takes me hours to walk to the Big House — there is hardly any room for my feet among the multitudes of flowers. My face is fixed in a silly grin, so happy am I to greet these old friends. "Hello, buttercup; nice to see you again, brodeia; pearly everlasting, I have missed you; blue-eyed grass, you are as lovely as ever." Each succeeding step brings me into a whole new realm of color. My attention is drawn deeper, deeper, closer, closer, until I am on hands and knees, my face bent to the earth, my eyes searching out this flower, then another then another. I am lost in the dimensionless world of the meadow's bloom, lost and transported by the wonder of it.

Never am I more aware of the richness that surrounds me here than in May. The bounteous variety of personality with which I come in daily contact astonishes me when I think of it. Each flower, each bird, even each cloud in the newly washed sky is distinct and unique; truly, my heart leaps, my spirit dances, my cup overflows.

This richness that I notice most in spring continues all year — to my continued, conscious delight if only I am receptive. Country life offers a multitude of events that are as graphic as May in their display of life's bounty. In its own way, the annual rabies clinic is one of these. The clinic is the county's effort to protect our pets — and by extension, us — from the perils of encountering a skunk that is foaming at the mouth. The incentive: cut rate on the shots and a chance to purchase a license for your dog at the same time.

Herry, an old friend from the city who has been living at the ranch this summer, and I draw clinic duty. I, because a near majority of the animals in question live with me; he, because he owns the only running car on the ranch today, and because — never having participated in this event — he doesn't object.

It is mid-August, the hottest time of year, and we have four dogs and three cats to transport the twenty dusty, curvy miles to the clinic. It's a situation made to order for a personality clash. The cats — Licorice, Lily, and Alisha — hiss and scratch any time they're within a quarter acre of each other, so clearly the only way to force them into the three-by-six-foot space of a car without bloodshed is to confine each one to a separate box. I scour the house for boxes that look durable enough to do the job and ask for help catching and securing the cats. It goes pretty well. Lily and Licorice are taken care of, I head off a last-minute escape by Alisha, then load the three boxes into the front seat of the car, making sure that the windows are closed to foil any further attempts at freedom.

Herry whistles for the dogs, all of whom except Jessica normally welcome a chance for a ride. They come running, tails wagging. But, uh-oh, we have a seating problem: Jojo and Sita are barely on speaking terms; neither wants to jump into a car where the other already is. But the problem is solved when All-Star and Jessica get in, climbing unnecessarily over the boxes of angry felines; Herry jumps in the back of the station wagon with Sita, holding her; I coax Jojo into the back seat; then Herry and I get out. The dogs settle down after a few leaps back and forth over the seat to establish territory and power and confusion.

Herry and I, already covered with dust and dog hair, not to mention cat scratches, run for our positions — he behind the wheel, me in the front seat, holding Alisha's box on my lap, with my elbow on Licorice's, and my feet keeping the lid on Lily's. Herry revs up Red Car's motor as we both say a silent prayer for no mechanical trouble today; then he turns up the driveway and down the dusty road.

Whew! What a day to have to keep the windows closed. Dog breath becomes oppressive; we crack the back windows, but a series of four Houdini-like escapes by Alisha keeps us from rolling down the front window. Lily starts to cry as we turn down the first curve, and with remarkable single-mindedness, continues complaining all the way. Licorice maintains a stony silence, but the odor from his box indicates that he has found another way to communicate his displeasure. Alisha continues to wiggle her way out of the most minute of cracks in her box.

The dogs are equally resourceful in their reactions to this unusual journey. Jessica begins to vomit about the same time that Lily starts crying, and she continues with matching single-mindedness, all the way down the road. Jojo and Sita leap back and forth between the seats, shadowboxing, canine style; All-Star looks out the window with commendable composure.

Herry drives like a careful fiend, trying to ignore the zoo operating on all sides. I fix my gaze on the road ahead, willing myself to ignore the queasy feeling that's rising in my stomach. After a very long hour, the dusty curves turn into a paved straightaway, and we are in town. I have directions to the vacant lot that is hosting the clinic, but since the first vehicle we see is a pickup with eight cow dogs in its bed following a Volkswagen with a St. Bernard in the front seat alongside a little old lady holding onto the leash of her brushed and bowed Pekinese, we realize that directions are quite unnecessary. We simply join the parade.

When we reach the lot where the clinic is set up, the scene immediately restores whatever part of our sense of humor had disappeared during the drive. The entire panorama is a caricature of itself: people — cowboys, Indians, children, housewives, teachers, hippies, businessmen — and their animals overflow the lot into the streets. A carnival spirit fills the air. Fat ladies with fluffy dogs, big men with little yappy dogs, cowboys with trucks full of range-bred working dogs. Little girls with three cats tucked under their arms, fancy ladies with Siamese cats in cages. A harried woman tugging helplessly along after a huge mongrel ("Slow down, Slowpoke," she pleads). Young boys trying to keep their mongrels on leash from leaping after the cats, who claw madly in their owners' arms to get away. Ranchers calling to each other from truck to truck, catching up on news. This is the biggest gathering since last summer's rodeo.

We get in line, and settle back to enjoy the show as we wait our turn. There's Andy with a pickup load of cow dogs, smile big as the sun. Herry goes over to pass some time with him, while I wait with our menagerie and decide not to worry about how we will get them all safely unboxed and presented to the vet, and then boxed again for the return trip.

I shift my attention from the circus to the star of the show, the young vet. He is right in the middle of the melee, cats and dogs threatening war over his shoulder and between his legs, and yet somehow he maintains his calm. He injects cat after dog after cat, gently, with a kind word to each.

And then he makes the rounds to the trucks, climbs into the fray of barking work dogs and, incredibly, emerges with shirt unmussed and dogs injected and quieted. We read in the paper the next week that 435 animals were vaccinated during the five hours of the clinic, but that raw statistic in no way conveys the heroism of the patient, unrumpled doctor.

And then it is our turn. Herry catches my frantic eye and returns to Red Car just as the vet arrives. Cats first, I think. Herry untangles the boxes from the front seat. I untie Licorice's box carefully, one hand prepared to grab at his anticipated dash for freedom. But he surprises me: after obligingly presenting thigh to needle, he pops quite willingly back into the box. Alisha and Lily, to our amazement and gratitude, follow suit.

This is a breeze, I think. Not to be outdone, the dogs leap out of the car on call, receive their shots, and hop back in. Nothing to it. Whoops. Where is Sita? There she is, hiding under the steering wheel, trying to ignore our calls for her appointment. Herry opens the door on the driver's side to make things easier for her, but she sees him coming and makes a dash for the back seat. A few more times back and forth, and we finally entice her to sit still in an accessible position in the car. The ever-accommodating vet reaches his arm through the window, places his final needle, says what a fine group of animals we have, and then it's done.

I take a deep breath of relief. The animals seem to register various feelings. Alisha glares at me out of the hole in her box, as if indignant to discover that the purpose of all this fuss was nothing more spectacular than a pinprick. All-Star just looks at me with her quiet brown eyes, evidently ready and willing to oblige me in whatever I might next ask her to do. And Jessica, though obviously still feeling the effects of her car sickness, responds to my relief with a lick and a tail wag. I give her a pat of gratitude in return.

[ 159 ]

Mission accomplished, Herry and I retreat to the air-conditioned local cafe, which is doing a booming business. Three iced teas and one chocolate malt later, it is time to hit the dust again. The return trip is a snap: Jessica seems to have nothing left inside to vomit, Lily has lost her voice, even Jojo and Sita settle for only a few rounds of musical seats. Alisha escapes from her box once more, emphatically, and I give in. She rides the last ten miles cradled in my arms, watching the trees pass.

Days later, I muse on the young vet's ability to quiet that crowd of excited animals. Not only had he remained calm in the face of the chaos, but he had also somehow communicated that calmness to the animals around him so that the potential free-for-all was transformed into an orderly and friendly process.

It seemed to me an extraordinary demonstration of the same communication I enjoy with Jessica. Invariably I know when she is hungry, thirsty, or wants to play — and she seems equally as aware of my moods of sorrow, exuberance, or fatigue. That kind of telepathy is, I think, not especially unusual for a dog and human who live so closely — but we are not used to expecting it in other interactions with the natural world.

Yet I sense it often in my life here. Part of the reason is that nature is teaching me. I find that living so intimately with animals alters my human-centered habits of interaction and perception. I pay less attention to words and more to gesture, tone, and feeling. When I am receptive, the animals seem to share with me perceptions beyond the range of my human limitations so that I can sometimes experience the world from the viewpoint of a creature with other gifts and interests than my own.

Thus, as I watch a hawk soar over the river canyon on the currents of the evening breeze, I begin to sense something of an aerial view of the land. And watching the ground squirrels search for food in the meadow, their efforts interrupted every two or three minutes by a check for danger, I taste the feeling of permanent caution.

Those little telepathies — for that is how they feel — are such a natural and normal part of life that I hardly notice what they indicate about my ideas of how the world is put together. But now and then something happens which so jolts my usual ways of thinking that I can only gasp. The story of one such experience starts at the end of our first summer.

In addition to the six horses of our ill-fated cattle deal, we also bought two beautiful Morgans from Allen, of the Horse Ranch, in our first months here. The mare, whom Debby named Madrone because her coat was red as the bark of the madrone tree, was good-natured and spirited and quickly became a favorite among both experienced riders and those, like me, who were still trying to learn how to walk around the meadow without losing control of the operation.

Late in September of that first year, while the summer heat was still in the air, Madrone got tangled in some of the stray barbed wire that cluttered the ranch, which we had tried to clean up but evidently had not yet conquered. Russell found her standing near the mailbox, her left hind leg torn into bloody strips by her efforts to disentangle herself from the wire. She was a terrible sight, clearly exhausted and weakened by her efforts, and in great pain from her wounds. We could see that the muscles and tendons were slashed, probably beyond repair, and the presence of pus and a disagreeable odor made a knot of fear form at the base of my stomach. But no one mentioned the word gangrene, or what people do to sick horses. Ranger drove up to the Horse Ranch to ask Allen to come take a look.

It didn't take him more than a few minutes to examine her leg and confirm our fear that she would have to be shot. We didn't question the decision; we realized that it was as wrenching for him as it was for us. She had been one of his favorite mares. Knowing that we were still novices in the ways of the country, he asked if we wanted to do it ourselves or if we'd like him to take care of it for us. Gratefully, we accepted his offer, and he drove back up the road to get his gun.

We led Madrone as best we could down into the meadow and tethered her, then went to the Big House for a gruesomely silent dinner. This was not the first animal that had died here — there was Horse A and also a baby deer we'd tried to keep alive — but Madrone had held a special place in all of our hearts, and her looming death seemed overwhelmingly senseless and unnecessary, caused by our own neglect in overlooking the human-made trap of barbed wire.

No one heard Allen's truck return, but suddenly our gloom was pierced straight through by a ringing shot that seemed to echo off the hills for minutes. Before anyone could get there, the truck drove away again, up the driveway toward home. Allen had come and done it, sparing us the necessity of being there; then he had gone before we could invite him for what could only have been a grief-stricken cup of coffee.

We buried lovely Madrone the next day in a shady place in the meadow, wishing her sweet eternal dreams of lush grass and open spaces.

The following spring, a full eight months after Madrone's death, I was sitting on the White House steps waiting for dinner. The sun was low in the sky, and a warm bronze color bathed the earth. Inside the White House were the sounds of dishes clattering in preparation for a meal and the voices of people gathering after a day of work. I sat alone, quietly, and my mind was far away, drinking in the peace of the final hours of the day.

Then my reverie was interrupted by the cows. The whole herd, thirty strong, was crossing the creek that runs by the White House, heading from the hayfield into the main meadow. The route was part of their normal one, but today something was disturbing their usual jostling, snorting movement.

Rastis, our friendly bull and director of the herd, was pawing a patch of ground and making a sound such as I had never heard before from a cow. A deep groan rose from somewhere in the depths of his several stomachs and burst into the still air with a retching heave. He seemed in deep distress. Saliva dripped from his chin and fell to the ground, which his front hooves continued to paw, now more frantically. Slowly the rest of the herd stopped its passage into the meadow and gathered around him. Several of the older heifers put their noses to the ground where he was pawing, and a few joined him with their own variations of that heart-wrenching groan.

The intensity of whatever was happening with the cattle completely magnetized the diffuse peace of the evening. All the suspended life of the meadow seemed to hover round their little circle, as if every element in creation had its attention riveted to that spot of earth. The feeling was too intense and consuming for me to have the mental space to worry about what was wrong. My energy, too, was drawn into the amazingly powerful focus that Rastis was creating, saliva dripping ever faster from his jaw, and unearthly sounds thrusting ever more insistently from his depths.

It continued for maybe fifteen minutes. And then suddenly I made the connection. The spot of earth that Rastis was pawing was precisely the spot upon which Madrone had been shot eight months before.

When Rastis finally began to calm, the pawing slowed down first, then the saliva stopped, and finally the moans became a whimper. He seemed not to notice the heifers gathered around him, but moved blindly through the herd, with the remnants of a cry still in his throat. He walked slowly, blinking, head hung low, past the heifers and into the meadow, alone. His cows watched, and then followed, without a sound.

The emotional impact of the cows' behavior was profound. First, the anguish of Madrone's death overwhelmed me once again. But then it passed, and in its place I felt an awesome sense of completion. Somehow the cows had performed the unfinished rites — though until that moment I hadn't been aware of the need for them. Finally I felt that Madrone had been properly mourned, by her fellow creatures, and that her spirit was at last released for another home.

I had no doubt that the cows' action was in response to Madrone's death, but realizing the connection raised more questions than it answered. From Rastis's point of view, what was he doing? Why had he waited eight full months after Madrone's death to do it — during which time surely any trace of scent of her blood would have been washed away by sun and rain? The cows had passed this spot almost daily since the night she was killed; why, this time, such a reaction? I still cannot answer those questions, but this event and others like it have shown me irrevocably that there are vast realms of life that lie beyond normal human understanding.

Our usual ways of thinking of life and death and individual uniqueness can't contain moments such as the cows' commemoration of Madrone. To me, that was a moving demonstration of a unity beyond the limits of time and space. The following April, I participated in another.

Spring is in the air. The breeze is gentle with the smell of birthing, the earth radiates freshness, the birds sing with more abandon than they have for months. The first wildflowers are in bloom in the deep forest: the hardy toothwort, the delicate purple shooting star. The tender green of new growth is everywhere. Grass has even sprouted through some cracks in the concrete of my floor: what better testament to life renewed?

I cannot stay inside. I gather up my quilt, pull back the blanket door, and venture forth.

The breeze plays with my hair as I make my way after an invisible pull toward the creek. On the southern slope of the hill that falls steeply to the stream, not far from the yurt, but out of sight, there is a tiny natural shelf in the hillside. I spread my quilt on the earth, which is still damp from winter rains.

The day is cool, but the slope is sheltered from the wind, and its angle catches the full power of the sun. I lie down, arms outstretched, motionless against the earth.

The earth molds itself to my curves: we fit. The sun reaches deep, through skin to bone, through surface to center. I smell the rich damp warmth of almost spring, see through my fingers and pores, listen with my bones, forget to breathe.

My attention is drawn to a small oak tree, not far from where I lie. Outlined against the clear blue sky, little bits of newborn green are barely visible on the tips of the gray moss-covered branches. Strings of Spanish moss drip toward the earth, dancing now and then in the breeze. A jay lands on a branch near me, cocks his head, and flies away again. The wind rises slightly; the whole tree responds, limbs swaying. Though my little

shelf is hidden from the wind, I seem to feel its push against me, too, as I watch the little oak.

I sense the branches moving, feel the creak of winter stiffness, feel new life begin to run through its body as the sun and wind pull and push. I feel the pull on kinky limbs, the sluggishness of parts still half asleep that respond only slowly to the call of the sun. I feel the breeze blow off the tree's winter coat and awaken something inside, deep within the core. And I sense the tree responding, branches swaying, bulky body moving slowly, sluggishly, as it can.

And then I *am* the tree. Another jay alights and I feel its touch as on a distant extremity. I am still here, still flat on the hillside hidden from the wind, but somehow I extend above and beyond and around myself to include the tree, the earth, the rocks, the breeze.

The earth, the rocks, the sky, and I interpenetrate. We are one. I feel a deep, beatific relaxation. The boundaries that I think of as "me" are suddenly no more than illusion. My body's limits are a product of the same surface tension that allows a water bug to skate on top of a pond. Now, as I lie here, the tension is released, the illusion suspended. The varied personalities and centers of energy that make up my place on the hillside merge, and all of life flows into and out of one another. And the many — the wonderful, entertaining, diverse manifestations of life — become gloriously One.

# XII

# No, Not Those Trees!

ONE SPRING afternoon in our first year, when I was still exploring places for the first time, I decided to climb the hill that towers over the ranch on our western border. My destination was a crag, which we call Windhook, that juts out on the southern slope nearly at the top of the hill.

As soon as I crossed the border of our land, the woods changed dramatically. I was suddenly in virgin forest, dwarfed by huge Douglas fir and yellow pine trees, many of them too big for me to encircle with my arms. I left behind the underbrush with which logging clutters the forest and found instead layer upon layer of oak leaves and pine and fir needles. I remember the smell: deep, pungent layers of dead plants and animals in the process of returning to the earth undisturbed. The sun found its way to the forest floor only in patches so that my path was mottled with light.

Once in the forest, my sense of direction was completely skewed by the huge trees that obscured familiar landmarks. I followed deer trails, which climbed the steep slope in zigzags, and figured that as long as I kept going up I would arrive somewhere eventually. The climb was hard and I had to stop often to catch my breath.

The forest was alive with wildlife. Bushy gray squirrels scampered before me, jays and juncos chattered from the tree branches, I could hear the distant tap-tap-tap of a woodpecker, and now and then I felt the hush of a deer's presence. I was struck by the rich sense of harmony in the undisturbed forest, and I realized that that sense was missing from the logged-over acres on the land within the ranch's boundaries.

As the sun was falling behind the hill, I broke out of the forest onto the rocky outgrowths. I found them steeper and narrower than they had appeared from the meadow; Windhook was barely wide enough for me to sit on. Perched on that narrow shelf, I could see all the way from Andy's land to the south, past Orvis's ridge to the north, and across the river to the mountains beyond. The land put itself together for me from that perspective better than it had from down below; I saw ridge flow into ridge and open out into meadow and watched everything tumble down into the canyon that the river carved. A feeling of spaciousness came over me; the ranch was a comfortable pocket in a larger and seemingly unending range of hills, meadows, forests, and valleys.

The ranch looked like a toy barnyard. The slope carried sounds to me so clearly that I could hear Ranger and Carol talking in the orchard, Russell calling for the cows, and all the other sounds of evening rising from the main houses. I began to feel uncomfortably like an eavesdropper.

I stayed until the sun went down and the moon rose, then made my way down the hill as best I could. Night noises, both strange and familiar, had overtaken the forest. The moonlight made its way to the forest floor as the sunlight had earlier; I wove through dappled shadows and finally reached the open spaces of home.

That hillside — the last piece of virgin forest for miles — is scheduled to be logged this summer. No more cushioned silence, no more thick wet humus, no more undisturbed natural harmony. No more deep green hillside, no more needled spears rising strong and straight into the last rays of the sun.

We had not expected this. We knew Louisiana-Pacific owned that hillside when we bought the ranch, but it had seemed a mistake on their part — too steep, too difficult, expensive and dangerous to cut. Even more important, it has been a long time since we have thought of those hills, or these, as "belonging" to anyone. They belong here, they grow here; they are the western wall of this valley we reside in. They shape our western horizon and are very much a natural part of this land that is the ranch.

By chance Michael met a Louisiana-Pacific survey team on the road today, and they told him logging was scheduled to begin in a couple of months. Despite the fact that nearby landowners are supposed to have a chance to comment on operations that may affect their own land, this was our first hint — and it was accidental — of L-P's intentions. It looks suspiciously like they had hoped to avoid alerting us and thereby giving us the time to challenge their plans legally.

Logging! Noise, bulldozers, chain saws, huge flatbed trucks leap into my mind. And suddenly I remember another day that same spring four years ago, another day of exploration.

It is early in March. The ground is still soaked with rain; winter's chill hangs in the air. But the season has clearly passed that unmistakable boundary into spring and we decide to have a picnic. With the efforts of establishing ourselves on the land still relatively new, we are not used to calling a vacation for a day, and we are slightly self-conscious. There are seven humans — Ashley, George, Annie, Susie, me, Bruce, and T. A. — four dogs, and two goats. The goats follow us from the houses across the main meadow and over the road as far as the sawmill site before turning back. T. A. rides on Ashley's shoulders, a blond towhead bobbing against the new-blue sky.

Ashley wants to show us a place he knows, a stream just this side of what we call the Middle Meadow. The waters run gurgling, bubbling with winter rainfall, through moss-covered rocks big enough to lean against. We play in the water and drink in the smell of damp moss.

We have brought a lunch. We are drawn from the dampness to the sunlight on the meadow, so steep here that we have to hold on to keep from sliding down into the gully below. George plays dog wth the dogs; Annie holds T. A. and they both laugh. We eat, sit together, talk a bit, and lie down in the not-yet-very-warm spring sunshine. Full of cheese sandwiches and apples, I drift off to sleep.

It's only a short nap, judging from the sun's place in the sky when I wake, but everyone else seems to have left. I roll over, groggy from sleep, and consider whether I will go back, too, or whether I'll call this a whole holiday and explore further. I'm still considering when I see a figure emerge from the forest's edge. It's Bruce, who decided halfway back with the others that what he really wanted to do was go to the Upper Meadow. That is all I need to hear; I'm going with him.

Together we climb the meadowed hill and turn south toward a grove of laurel trees. I have never been in just this part of the meadow before, and after my nap, it all has an ethereal, unreal quality, as if I were seeing through haze. Neither of us feels like talking. We wander, silent, just looking, immersed in our separate thoughts.

The grove of laurel trees hides a spring, bubbling out of the dark wet earth between more mossy rocks. I stoop to drink and then continue, climbing again, still heading south. The meadow opens out once more, and we climb to outgrowths of rock, from which we can see the county road below; the meadow stretches wide on either side of us. Suddenly we hear horses' hooves, coming fast, and the whoosh of wind stirred up by galloping bodies. We see them, the entire herd, running down the hill from the Upper Meadow, manes flowing, tails streaming, ears laid back. As they come closer we can see the wildness in their eyes. Is someone or something chasing them? Or?

Just as it seems that they will run past without seeing us, Princess, the lame Shetland pony who was on the land when we moved here, wheels on her crippled legs and gallops directly at us. Unable to do anything else, too startled to call or jump out of the way, we watch, fascinated, as the dust-colored pony, still fuzzy with her winter coat, runs right at us. Barely three feet short of running us down, she stops abruptly, her nostrils quivering, her flanks heaving. She stares for a full minute, then turns as abruptly as she came, and gallops back to join the rest of the pack, who are already stirring clouds of dust on the county road.

Before we have time to figure out what spooked the horses, we hear it. The noise. We hear it, and look at each other, and run: down the hill, back toward the familiar, friendly main meadow, without a word. We run, without looking back, not the way the horses ran, but back the way we came, through laurel grove, over stream, down steep hill, on the county road, past the sawmill, home. Panting, we sit down together to catch our breath. Only then do we speak.

"What was *that*?" I ask Bruce.

"What did you hear?" he finally responds.

[ 173 ]

"Caterpillars, big bulldozers, huge machinery, mowing down children, cows, everything in their way, cutting into the earth. Squeals, grinding of engines. I heard bodies being tossed up into the air."

Silence. "Well?" I said. "What did you hear?"

"The same."

I think of that day now, never adequately explained by what was going on at the ranch within earshot. All we could come up with was that the sounds must have come from a nearby ranch. But the striking, uncanny similarity of our mental images of what we heard? No reasonable explanation for that.

Tonight, with the full shock of the projected logging just beginning to sink into my mind, that afternoon seems like a piece of the future. A warning of what was to come.

I think of what it will mean if they cut the hill. Bulldozers, chain saws, winches, whining, grinding, groaning, moaning, morning till night, day after day. Roads cut into the hillside, streams diverted and maybe polluted, slash and beer cans lying everywhere. Animals, plants, birds uprooted, nature's balance violently overturned in a few short weeks. A war enacted on the hillside, bodies left wounded, bleeding, dying slow, protracted deaths. No wonder there was wild fear in Princess' eyes.

Dinner is grim, filled with powerless anger, not yet turned to thinking of what, if anything, we can do. I walk out into the meadow with Ellen, Carol's younger sister, who has been living on the ranch for a year now, long enough to have developed a passionate love for the land. The moonlight glistens in the tears on her face. Anger, hopeless rage, despair, tears. I am surprised at the intensity of my feelings: I can feel the bulldozers crawling over me, hear the chain saw drilling in my ear, feel the crash of a still-living tree onto unsuspecting life below. I had not realized just how intimate my relationship with the land had become, so that the intended assault on the hillside feels like a violation of something vital in me. The magnitude of the realization of what is going to happen hits me — and all of us — like a thunderbolt, hits us all at our hearts, in our guts, way beyond the reach of reason, convention, or "reality." It hits like a draft notice, and we react like a mother: no, not my son, no, no matter what the cause. No, not those trees, no, they are a part of me.

It's not quite that simple, of course. Many of us live in wood houses; all of us use tables, chairs, and shelves made from dead trees. I have learned here that death is part of life, and I need not shrink from taking life for what I really need. But I have also learned that nature's laws are sacred and precise, and the balance of give and take cannot be ignored without penalty. Sites like the one alongside the ranch pose real problems for the careful logger. It takes time and money on such a steep slope to prevent soil erosion and damage to watershed. So much time and money that it cuts into profit, and it seems likely that on this and other hillsides, nature's balance will come up short.

The real problem here, or one large dimension of it, is that this is steep watershed land that never should be logged. The present need to log here results from decades of short-sighted practices. Easily accessible, rolling hillsides were cut and never replanted. Those were the places (including many square miles of public forests) where logging could have been done without excessive damage to the forests, soil, and water. Reforestation would have worked there. But in their haste to get on to the next cutting, the loggers and foresters neglected to plant the trees. The logging companies were motivated by short-term profits, and the U.S. Forest Service and other agencies whose job it was to regulate the logging industry, but whose directors, in practice, were basically agents for timber profiteering, violated the public trust.

After decades of this abuse, some of the world's greatest forests have been reduced to small enclaves of virgin timber in steep, vulnerable mountain watersheds. Trees we plant now will take more than thirty years to reach saw-timber size under the most favorable conditions. The timber industry "needs" to cut the remaining virgin growth because it abused our public and private forests for decades. Now we *all* have a problem to face. We must evolve a way to balance our needs harmoniously with the earth's gifts, and in the short term we must somehow pay for this legacy of human greed and disregard in the timber industry, which is, we must remember, not different from our own greed and disregard.

Many levels of our lives and efforts seem to converge. Our relationship to the land, our relationship and responsibility to the world, our struggle to act in harmony with nature's laws; the story that has been enacted on this land, our budding life with it, our hopes and dreams for the future of this and all land. It all comes together, layer upon layer: experience, emotion, reason, hope; past, present, future. And out of it comes a very clear mandate to act. The projected logging stimulates a connection, experience and feeling flow into conviction, and we start to map a course of action.

What can we do? Louisiana-Pacific is required to submit a Timber Harvest Plan to the State Department of Forestry before their operation can begin. We, the public, have the right to file objections to that plan if the proposal affects our rights or well-being. With the April wildflowers just beginning to take over the meadow, we ask for and receive a copy of the plan.

The Harvest Plan more than ignores the existence of our ranch. Despite the fact that the survey team spoke with Michael, that they have driven past our visibly operating ranch in order to get to their land, that it is impossible for anyone to walk on the hillside in question — as they have — without looking directly down upon our garden, hayfield, orchard, cows, horses, people, and two main houses, the Harvest Plan specifically denies that we are here.

"Is any water for domestic use taken within or not more than 100 feet downstream of your proposed area of operation? . . .

yes__ no _x_ "

The blatant errors in the plan are actually in our favor, since they will help us buy some time to study our rights and means of appeal.

We hire an attorney to help us understand our legal rights as citizens and water users and to represent us at the public hearing which we hope to have. George, James, and Michael climb into a car and go to Sacramento. They try to see the governor, and succeed in meeting with the Director of the State Resources Department and then with her assistant, who in turn contacts the forester who will be reviewing the Harvest Plan to advise him of the errors and to speak on our behalf.

Our biggest concern is the effect the logging might have on our water supply. Our three major water sources originate on that hillside; any damage to the watershed will seriously affect our well-being and the future of agriculture, livestock, and life on the ranch. We contact the California Water Quality Control Board for help, information, and a personal inspection. The board's representative supports our conclusion that the plan as submitted would damage our water supply and therefore endanger ranch operations. This is May 9.

With the report of the Water Quality Control Board in hand, the Forestry Department refuses approval of the plan as originally submitted on May 23. A public hearing, ostensibly to allow us and Louisiana-Pacific to "come to terms," is set for June 5.

We are pleased with our progress to date; we have succeeded in establishing ourselves as concerned and active citizens and landowners; we have earned the right to be heard. But we have won nothing yet. We put all our energies toward preparing for the hearing.

This is logging country. It is unpopular, and maybe even dangerous, to stand in the way of the major source of employment for local people. We tighten up our thinking, debate among ourselves. We want to do our homework meticulously, so that our neighbors and friends will hear true and honest concern in our arguments and not react against us instinctively as rabble-rousing, heartless, idealistic environmentalists who care nothing for where they get their next house payment.

We call in soil specialists and a geologist, ask for the advice of ecology groups, read up on soil erosion and the Forestry Act. Our lawyer comes up for two days and a night; we ask questions, walk over the land, and plan. According to our attorney, it would be nearly impossible to stop the logging completely. With a great deal of money — which we don't have — for legal nitpicking, we might be able to force repeated delays, but winning a total halt of the operation is highly unrealistic. He counsels us to aim instead at a correction of the errors of the original plan and some agreement to mitigating environmental protective measures by L-P.

All right. We draw up some compromise measures which, if strictly adhered to, ought to protect our water and temper the environmental impact. We ask for a buffer zone around the streambeds, within which no trees would be cut; the installation and maintenance of culverts on permanent roadways; and an agreement to leave 30 percent of the healthy conifers as seed trees outside of the buffer zones.

We also meet the local contractor who will do the actual cutting for L-P. He impresses us as a decent, conscientious man, who lives on a ranch of his own and seems to have real feeling for the land. Inquiries around town support his reputation for careful work. We are relieved to think that the logging will at least be a clean operation.

June 5, the day of the hearing, arrives. A clear, warm, sunny day. We all put on our city clothes, Bruce cuts his hair, we slip into our best behavior. The hearing is three hours away; we plan our arrival to have plenty of time to wipe away the dust.

From our standpoint, the crucial detail of this meeting is to determine where the roads will be. If they are at the easiest, obvious crossing of the streams, they will be too close to our land, irrigation reservoirs, and domestic water intake. If they are almost anywhere else, the crossings are prohibitively steep: too expensive for L-P, and likely to dump half the hillside into our water systems. The difficulty in road placement makes it seem nearly impossible to harvest this hillside without grave damage to our water supply or to corporate profits.

Louisiana-Pacific has sent officials and experts armed with a revised Harvest Plant which admits, without explanation or apology, the errors of the original and offers some compromise proposals. The L-P regional manager summarizes their argument, using a tiny photocopy map with thick felt pen lines to illustrate their intentions. It is impossible for us to tell, from that map, exactly where the roads will go.

We have made and hung up a large map, drawn to scale. When L-P finishes its presentation without clarifying the question of road placement, Bruce presses the regional manager to specify where the roads will go on the map that we have brought. The regional manager declines. Bruce objects, for he has realized that since there is no question period scheduled, this is our only chance for public answers to the crucial questions. Then the presiding State Forester rules Bruce out of order. So much for any real communication.

Instead, it is our turn for a presentation. Ellen reads her carefully prepared brief that submits our compromise proposals; James speaks of our agricultural pursuits, present and future; Bruce talks about the misrepresentation of facts in the Harvest Plan and the ethical negligence of Louisiana-Pacific.

The hearing as thus structured effectively inhibits any interaction between us and the L-P officials. Theoretically, both we and they are presenting our arguments to the presiding officer, who will then make a decision on the basis of all the evidence. But we never feel that our objections are really being heard by the State Forester who is presiding. Rather, it seems that we are a nuisance that must by law be dealt with and that those in charge are dealing with us as superficially and quickly as possible. Why can we not even get an answer to the crucial question: where will the roads go? What is the purpose of the hearing if such a basic concern is left unanswered?

We do the best we can under the circumstances, and in two hours the hearing is over. The State Forester promises a decision within a week. With heavy, troubled hearts, we head for home.

A week later we receive notification that the errors in the original plan have been corrected and some mitigation measures granted, though not quite what we had asked for. For example, rather than acceding to our request for a buffer zone of 100 feet on either side of the stream beds, within which no trees would be cut, the decision allows L-P to cut 50 percent of the trees within the buffer zone but stipulates that no machinery can be used and that the trees must be cut to fall away from the stream. L-P also offers to help us redesign our water system, and maybe even to loan us some machinery for the job: a thin offer, we feel, considering the impact of what they are about to do and their efforts to avoid negotiating with us about it.

We consider pursuing the matter legally but are advised, as before, that our chances of gaining anything substantial are very small and any further action will be very expensive. Instead, our lawyer recommends that we document the entire projected logging operation as completely as possible, in order to keep public pressure on L-P, force them to keep to the agreements of the Harvest Plan, and collect information for a potential lawsuit if they do not live up to their promises.

The possibility of a damage suit is small comfort, but we compile information and make sure that L-P knows we are still actively concerned. We take water samples from all the streams, continue personal contact with the contractor, take photographs of the watersheds. The Water Quality Control Board agrees to watch the proceedings and hear any complaints. Ellen writes to the State Department of Resources Director, relating our experience and asking that the department be aware of the action of its State Foresters and aid the public in enforcing the Forest Practices Act. Bruce writes to the California Department of Forestry, registering our protest at the hearing procedure and the decision that came out of it.

Meanwhile, the trees stand proud and tall to the sky, the eagles sit on their hatching eggs, the squirrels scamper in and out of the changing light, and the deer glide sleek and unseen through the deep, dark forest.

The bulldozers, chain saws, and flatbeds are scheduled to arrive in four to six weeks.

One day in mid-June, not long after hearing the final verdict from the State Forester, I walked alone to the river. Thinking and talking about the projected logging had raised some troublesome questions of conscience for me, and I realized how far short we, too, fall from acting in true harmony with nature's balance. With heightened awareness, I notice the impact of our human presence on this land — the meadow that is becoming over-grazed, the piles of cans waiting to be separated for recycling, the little bits of plastic that disintegrated last year before we boxed them and took them to the dump. The greed and carelessness that make us think we are in just a little too much of a hurry to take the time to do it right the first time are really different only in scale from the corporate greed and carelessness that will harvest this hillside.

Today I realize how far civilization has taken us from the natural awareness of life's interdependence that ruled the hearts of more primitive people. The day matches my mood: it is dark and stormy, strange for June. The river is high and gray, swept by a chilly wind. I sit for hours on a big rock at the water's edge, huddled in my jacket. I watch the clouds chase each other across the sky, watch the whirlpools swirl in angry waters.

Slowly, slowly, but inevitably, the noise in my head diminishes, and the sound of the river enters in. I am grateful. My mind feels fuzzy, weary, half-conscious.

My eye catches a tick crawling along the arm of my jacket. It is a common red-bodied tick that probably dropped on me from above as I walked through the forest. Without thinking, I pluck it from my sleeve and flick it into the water. My eye stays with it absentmindedly as the current catches it and pulls it toward the frothing waters in the middle of the river.

Suddenly the haze disappears, the veil lifts from my mind, and I *see* the tick. I see the creature that is struggling helplessly in the cold, churning water. I flash back to a childhood fear of being thoughtlessly, casually, crunched by a giant. My consciousness identifies with the tick, and I feel myself swirled ever faster, around and around, terrified. I feel myself panic, fight the tumbling waters helplessly, beyond any reason, guided only by a desperate and hopeless drive to survive.

The figure on the rock, giant-human-me, looms large, dark, and stupid. Jolted (but . . . I didn't mean . . . if I had only known . . . if I had thought), I reach forward, try to take him back. But it is too late. The tick is beyond my grasp, already on his way toward the sea. I have a glimpse of a terror-stricken, lingering, reasonless death. I watch in horror and humility and the lesson echoes in my heart.

*Epilogue:* It turned out that L-P didn't log Windhook that summer. The contractor informed us in early July that he'd been assigned another job because there was a surplus of logs at the mill where these trees would have been delivered. To us, that was a particularly intriguing explanation, which confirmed our suspicion of the entire preharvest procedure; at the hearing just a month earlier, we had all listened to the foreman of that same mill testify that without the logs from Windhook the mill would have to shut down for the summer and all those jobs would be lost. It was hard to see that testimony now as anything other than an outright lie.

But we hardly cared about such details — Windhook was not to be cut! Despite the fact that the halt came from none of our efforts, we were overcome by a sense of victory. Another year to watch the sun sink behind a fir-pierced horizon seemed a miraculous reprieve. Perhaps we could figure out a way to stop it forever before the next summer.

But when the next summer arrived, there had been no change in the logging laws, no new procedures that we could use to force a final pause. The logging proved to be every bit as shattering of life and peace on the hillside as we had feared. The bulldozer, chain saws, and double-axle trucks arrived and determined our dawn-to-dusk reality seven days a week for eight weeks. From the yurt it sounded like the trees were landing on my roof, and I never became accustomed enough to the awful groan and thud of a tree falling that my stomach ceased to turn over when I heard it.

The local contractor had been given the authority to cut only half of the hillside because of the continuing surplus at the local mill, an edict that slashed his profits, since he still had the expense of moving his entire operation to Windhook but the opportunity for only half as much timber to sell. He did a careful job. But the fears about this being a difficult hillside to harvest carefully were tragically justified by three serious accidents that happened to his crew, which had previously had a superior safety record.

The roads were built, as we had feared, across the streams that provide our domestic water. Two of the three winters following the logging have been drought winters, with lighter-than-normal rainfall, so it hasn't been easy to determine the full effects of soil erosion. The White House water seems muddier after a heavy rain, but long-term changes are thus far hard to measure.

That, in a larger sense, is the real irony and frustration of the legal process. In order to do what we could to protect Windhook, we found ourselves drawn into a negotiation of technicalities that were beyond our understanding or our real intention — and perhaps beyond those of the foresters as well. I wonder whether it is really possible to safeguard the health of a forest by determining the size and character of a buffer zone. Anyone who has seen a hillside that has been logged knows that the effects of such a trauma are drastic and long-term and are marked not only by the loss of the great trees, but also by subtle and far-reaching changes in soil and plant and animal life.

The effects on our lives of the logging of Windhook are not yet fully known. But there is no question that life on that hillside has been permanently altered. The natural processes of growth and death in the forest have been shaken by extreme human intervention, and it would be foolish to think that we who live so close will avoid a taste of the aftershocks.

# XIII

# "You Are Afraid"

BEFORE WE moved here, someone told us that the first winter would be the hardest test. If we made it through to spring, life in the country was supposed to be clear sailing. But in our case, the first summer was such an all-out assault that we welcomed the fall rains with relief, and the winter that followed brought slow and needed healing. The pattern established then has more or less continued: summers are our hard times.

One reason is that summers here are very hot. It is not uncommon for temperatures to reach 115 degrees in the shade during the intermittent hot waves. In heat like that, nothing really matters or exists except survival. On the hottest days, the sun smolders from the moment it breaks loose from the horizon and by 10 a.m. has reduced all life, including human, to its lowest common denominator.

Heat of that intensity is with for only three or four days a stretch. But it lurks always, threatening at the edges of more normal 90- to 100-degree temperatures. And in California there are no summer thunderstorms to release the tension. Summer on the ranch is a seemingly endless succession of sun-bleached days broken by cool, star-strewn nights.

I have learned to love the feeling of being baked and purified by the fire in the sky. But the glare can be harsh, its aura unbalancing, and its intensity a catalyst for seeds of change planted or inhibited in less exacting seasons.

Summer is time of activity — gardening, construction, fencing, canning. Other summers we have willfully intensified the pressure with hay hauling contracts or summer camps. This year we have tried to take the edge off the season by just living: weeding the garden, fixing the cars, caring for ourselves and the animals. It is a good try. But, as if in defiance of my determination to be calm, cool, and collected, I feel summer sneaking up on me when it is least expected. I am ill at ease, strange to myself. I fight against it, rail against it, unwilling; but the uneasiness still comes, bubbling up around the edges, throwing me off my so carefully planned balance.

I spent all day yesterday baking bread and cleaning up the Big House. When I walked in this morning, the sink was full of dirty dishes, six of the eight loaves of bread were gone, and flies swarmed over the basket of garden vegetables on the porch. There was jam smeared on the table, obscured by another cloud of flies. Yesterday's newspaper was strewn over the dining room table and chairs amidst a T-shirt, one work glove, a ragged pair of jeans, and a cowboy hat. I felt my neck muscles tighten, my face draw into a frown, my shoulders bend with the weight of the ranch upon them. Damn communal living! This place is always a mess! Why can't anyone remember to pick up a sweater or fold the newspaper? Or to wash a dish or wipe off the counter? I stomped out of the house, slamming the door behind me, and noted that the hinge still needed repair.

There must be an easier way. Why didn't I marry that nice young man who was going to be a lawyer? By now he is probably neatly established in a clean white frame house with two clean and obedient children and a car that runs and a screen door that closes. What am I doing here, in a kitchen that's a perpetual mess, in a commune that's impossible to regulate, in a place where there is always something that needs vital attention and everything is screaming to be done?

I remembered a Christmas card I received last year from a college friend who married a doctor, had a two-year-old child, was starting graduate school, and lived in the suburbs. "When things get ridiculously hectic around here, I think of you," she wrote, "with your peaceful and sane country life." "Peaceful and sane?" I thought. Ha! Life in graduate school, with a home in the suburbs, seems the definition of sanity to me right now.

I stormed across the porch and jumped to the ground, still grumbling to myself. But there at my feet was Jessica, tail wagging so hard her whole body shook. And by her side was Jojo, prancing in delight at my presence. In the face of such resolute cheerfulness, I had to smile, first at the dogs and then at myself. What was I thinking of anyway, to get caught in that old trap? Life must be more peaceful in grad school, indeed. And the grass a lot greener, too, no doubt.

I reached down to give the dogs a friendly shove. "C'mon, you two," I said. "Race you to the river."

After two laps of the river's pools I have forgotten my frustration at this morning's dirty kitchen. I skim down the rapids, then paddle lazily over to the big rock to lie in the sun. Nestling into a compatible curve in the stone, lulled by the sound of the water moving easily toward the sea, I fall into a dream-filled sleep. The dogs sleep nearby.

When I awake, a shadow has come over the river. The sun is low in the sky and the day's air is finally cool, but the rock is still warm. Feeling like a reptile, I move to an area more recently touched by the sun. While I thumb through my dreams, I mold myself flat on the rock's contours,

[ 189 ]

soaking up the warmth the sun has stored within it during all the hot hours of the day. As the sky loses its daytime brilliance, the vultures take over the space way above me with their dancing, weaving patterns. I stay until the evening breeze makes me shiver. Then, with the dogs, I pick my way across the rocks to my clothes on the other side of the river. I dress, and, in the gathering dusk, we climb the bank to the path up the hill.

The gathering dusk. Suddenly I understand that phrase. The air is thick with the assembling forces of the night. And as I step onto the dirt path, I feel a strange sensation come upon me, from inside and out, from my bones to the frame of my skin.

I am afraid.

I recognize it with a shock, unused to feeling fear in the woods. Yet the feeling is unmistakable. And my skin is covered with goosebumps. Afraid of what? I wonder. I want a focus for my fear, to explain and justify the feeling to myself. I decide I must be afraid of rattlesnakes.

Dusk is a likely time for snakes to be out hunting and drinking after the dangerous heat of the day is past, and I could easily come upon one unexpectedly in this semi-darkness. Suddenly every stick seems to be moving. I place each foot with conscious care, eyes glued to the ground, and ears cocked for the slithering sound of snake moving through leaves and grass. The breeze rustles the leaves of a bush to my right: I leap away from the sound.

Then I begin to be truly afraid. I know enough about the power of fear and thought to know that they often attract their objects. I do not want to inadvertantly create the situation I think I fear. I stop, and force myself to take a deep breath. Rattlesnakes are too simple an explanation for the feeling that overwhelms me, anyway. I give up my need for a focus reluctantly, but the fear remains.

All my senses are hyperalert. I walk without a sound, trying to be invisible, to pass through without being noticed. Yet I feel conspicuous in my silence. Darkness is full upon the forest by now. The night creatures are out, and they and the forest celebrate the return of darkness with song. All creation seems to be singing: the trees, swaying in the night wind; the tall grasses, rustling by the stream; the thistles, catching on my jeans as I pass. The crickets and frogs keep up the background rhythm, the voices of bats and an owl carry the melody. In the distance a coyote sings a solo. There are other voices that I cannot identify.

In the vast symphony of sound, my silence sticks out more pointedly than if I had screamed. I feel agonizingly out of place, as if in a terrifyingly foreign country. I know not a word of the language. Yet I feel clearly that I have to speak, to join in the music, or else I have no right to be here.

I begin to hum, softly, with no melody in mind. My voice sounds thin and unsteady. Determined to try to master my fear, I squat near a pool in the stream that is making its way to the river. I stay for a while, humming softly all the time, taking my cues from the air, trying to blend my song with the melody of the water. I feel a brief flash of acceptance, long enough to lift the mantle of fear from my heart for just a moment; but as soon as I register what has happened, the moment vanishes. Once again I become a clumsy, fearful human in a place where I do not belong.

I pull myself up the long hill toward home. All around me, I smell animal: musky, wild, big, free animal. Bear, coyote, racoon, mouse, owl. I do not see them except by their smells, but I feel them seeing me, impatient for me to pass.

At the top of the hill, at the tail end of the forest before the path winds into open meadow space, I stop. The spooky feeling is still with me and I do not want to go home afraid. I want to understand this feeling. I sit down on the path, my face to the trees. I sit, watch, listen, smell, and try to understand.

It is an uncommon night for early August: the wind has a distinctly autumn flavor. I watch the wind blow down the river canyon, tossing the tree branches against the pale gray sky. I listen to the trees creaking, hear their branches rubbing against one another, listen to their screeches and moans. I look up. The trees dance above me, leaping and swooping in the night air. I have a moment of panic: what is to keep them from falling down upon me, from crushing me? An owl calls softly behind me. Shivers run down my back.

I do not move a muscle. I make myself stay. The wind continues up and down the canyon, the trees continue their eerie dance. The night animals are on their way to hunt and be hunted. There is an order here, a familiarity, a sense that this is the way things are in the night. It is all in place. And it all goes on without me. I am superfluous, an alien.

It no longer matters whether or not I have an answer for my fear. I know it is time to go.

As I walk onto the meadow, I determine to leave the dark path and its fears behind me. An uneasy night leads into another brilliantly hot summer day, and then another, and still another. I fall once again into my summer patterns, and the strange walk up from the river is all but buried in the continuing force of the moment. I rise, I meditate, I write; I try to stay cool; I weed the garden, help Carol make dinner, read Josie a bedtime story. And then I do it all again, not quite the same, yet not quite differently.

But something is off. Patterns that are usually harmonious seem tedious now; simple daily tasks have become burdens; I am restless, impatient. I find myself thinking of rattlesnakes obsessively; I hardly take a step without wondering if there will be a snake at the end of it. Everyone and everything seem to irritate me. I want to go away and hide.

Instead, I decide to go to the wilderness.

The ranch is a day's walk from the border of the National Forest's wilderness area. The wilderness land is kin to ours, drawn from more unruly stock. The rocks are bigger, the animals more numerous and less accustomed to human neighbors, the waters colder and more headstrong. My destination is on the fringe of the wilderness area, where one of the largest tributaries joins another fork of the same river that runs by the ranch. It is a place that strikes familiar notes, but pushes them to the unknown.

A few miles above the river, I encounter a small rattlesnake, not more than a foot long. I hear or sense him rather than see him, so perfectly does he blend with the fir-needle-strewn forest. My foot stops just short of stepping on him. He moves slowly to the edge of the path and turns to stick out his tongue at me.

Determined as I am to take courage and positive thinking into this week, I try to pretend that my knees are shaking from relief. Now that the snake I have been watching for all summer has finally appeared — in miniature — surely I should be able to laugh at my obsession. But I can't quite pull it off. I know that the bite of this baby rattler is every bit as powerful as that of his grandfather, and his appearance in reduced size is no cause for comfort. I walk past him hurriedly and try to ignore the fear that prickles the back of my neck.

The incident passes quickly, or more likely I bury it quickly in the predominant harmony of the virgin fir forest. The stillness soothes me, reaches out to my battered spirit, until I sense the borders of that peace that waits beyond words, beyond human interaction. Stillness, peace, wordless energy: this I need, I have come to find.

I lope down the last steep hill to the confluence of the rivers where I will camp. I lay my pack on the sandy beach on my side of the point and walk to the water's edge. With the exception of this beach, the river meets land as far as I can see in a profusion of huge boulders, many of them more than twice my height and as wide as they are high. The boulders are pink, orange, white, and bright green; their presence contributes to the deep, bouncing echo of this steep canyon and to the feeling of insignificance I have as I survey it.

I reach down to test the deep green water and find that it is cold enough to numb, in contrast to the river by the ranch, which is placid, warm, and shallow this late in the season. Here are pools still deep enough to dive into, water running swiftly enough to foam white over rapids.

The land rises sharply above the boulders, in thick forest and sheer rock, 500 feet or more to the sky. High above me on the tributary side of the gorge are the piles of an old footbridge — the only sign I can see of human presence, and that long ago destroyed by the force of nature. I feel far from home, not especially welcome here, and uncomfortably human. I want to melt in among the boulders, glide through the river waters without making a ripple — but I can't seem to walk across a rocky shore without making a racket.

Uneasiness floods me momentarily, but I manage to contain the feeling by turning to set up camp and make dinner. Once my little fire is crackling into the approaching night and my pot of rice is suspended over the flames, bubbling cheerily, I am reassured. After dinner I scrub the pot with river sand, watch the fire die slowly, and climb gratefully into my sleeping bag, savoring the touch of the earth underneath.

I wake early, before the sun has turned the sky's morning gray to blue. All uneasiness of the day before is gone and I feel a tingle of anticipation as I roll my sleeping bag and start a fire for fir-needle tea. I am here where I should be and I am going to do what I must. I have definite conscious goals for the week: to clear out the psychic babble in my head, to relax, to meet the faceless fear which has been plaguing me all summer. This first morning, seven days seems like plenty of time for those tasks. I am ready and eager to begin.

My first feeling is relief. I have nothing to do. Nothing I have to do. I have time to let my thoughts go, take their own shape, reclaim their truth. I lie lazily among the boulders, mold my body to their shape, soak their warmth into my bones. When the sun gets hot, I roll into the shade or slide into the clear, cold water. I swim back and forth and around the pool, watching my shadow glide along the river bottom, watching the sun play through the water on my body. The river soothes me, the exercise feels good. I am slowly cleansed.

I indulge my moods. I read for hours without stopping, scribble notes now and then, fall asleep in the sun. I walk down the river, hopping from boulder to boulder, balancing along a fallen tree, wading in shallow water. I know there must be many steelhead caught in the deep pools, waiting for the fall rains to carry them to the sea, but I see none. There are signs of bear everywhere. But I see nothing moving, no one. I feel overpoweringly, deliciously, and frighteningly alone.

In my journal I write: "First day, hard to 'stop.' Restless, anxious. Second day, easier. By evening, I live here. Third day, I stop counting days, fall into the rhythm: feels good."

My mind twitches and jerks like an overused muscle. It doesn't seem to want to relax. To coax it along, I try imitating the state of pure "being" I've so often watched in the dogs. Their procedure is to find a proper place, adjust themselves comfortably, attend to pressing business such as flea scratching, and then, presto, to "be" — seemingly for as long as they choose. Their eyes are usually half-closed, but their ears and noses are obviously alert. It is a meditative state, not a withdrawal from the world, but a total entering into it.

This morning in the sunlight, I try a human version of that state. Settled on the top of a boulder that is deep green and streaked with pink, I gaze at the river below. I let the thoughts come and usher them through and out, trying not to think of them as mine. I let the river lull me, let it envelop me, try to lose myself within it. I feel my head relax, watch my thoughts dance in the sunlight, then almost, almost, let go. . . .

Slightly past the midpoint of the week, my thoughts turn to the bizarre. Accidents, sickness, madness, sad memories intrude on my peace. Is this what happens to people who are alone too long? I wonder. Yet I know that my thoughts are not the product of wilderness solitude, but rather part of the mental noise I brought with me. The longer I am away from society's taboos, the less restraint my mind exercises. I feel slightly crazy, released in some ways, but also adrift in unknown and scary waters.

By the fifth day I can no longer read the books I have brought with me; I have had enough of words. I lie, just lie in the sun for hours. My mind spins off, drifts lazily, stumbles. A feeling of panic washes over me: a nameless, faceless panic. Am I slipping away from myself? Or is something creeping up on me?

The last whole day to be here, I wake up anxious. The peace of the week suddenly seems false, contrived. I have not accomplished my primary purpose yet, and I know it. That unknown fear I have felt all summer is still lurking over my shoulder. I have not yet looked it in the face, and I cannot leave until I do. And then I remember my dream.

I am walking on a beautiful hillside. Birds are singing, deer peek out from between the trees, the sky is a deep, clear blue. I am dressed in a flowing white robe, with a halo of flowers in my hair. In the distance I can hear the gentle gurgle of a stream. The scene looks like paradise. But I am racked with anguish: my stomach is churning, turning, knotting in agony. "What's wrong with me?" I cry. "Why do I ache so?" And from nowhere, a voice answers: "You are afraid of dying."

Remembering this now, I realize that my stomach is still churning. And then the voice comes back clearly — deep, resonant, and commanding. "You are afraid of dying."

Am I? I don't think so, not particularly. No more than most people.

Suddenly I am furious, completely overcome by a blinding anger. I pull on shoes and clothing, throw my sleeping bag in the direction of my pack, and plunge across the slippery rocks and white water to the steep, sheer cliff that has loomed over me all week.

Without a moment's hesitation or thought I start to climb. The rock crumbles in my grip, my feet slip, I scrape my knee in sliding. I grab for something solid, will myself forward and upward, strain for a foothold. I pull on a small tree, and it comes off in my hand; I catch myself on a rock to keep from falling.

Fifty feet off the ground, then seventy-five. I look down once, and a glimmer of the extent of my foolhardiness flickers in my mind. Below me is hard rock, and help is miles away. But my anger is undiminished; I continue to climb.

My body presses almost flat against the rock, inching, squirming, and writing ahead. Sweat makes my fingers slippery; as I lose my grasp of a slick old root, I slide down ten feet fast enough to catch the dislodged dirt and gravel in my hair and eyes and mouth. I pause to catch my breath, spit out the cliff's debris, and then move up again.

Three hundred feet above the river, the cliff face falls slightly from the perpendicular, and the rock becomes jagged enough to accommodate scrub oak and manzanita. It is not yet so flat that I can walk upright, though, and as I crawl through the rocks and occasional clumps of grass, I note the likelihood of running into a rattlesnake. To my surprise, the thought evokes not fear, but defiance.

I make an attempt to move carefully, but I am not in control of my muscles. My mind races with thoughts; I cannot think logically. What if I get lost? I weave my way on hands and knees through a tangle of low-growing manzanita; I have completely lost my sense of direction, know only that I must climb as long as there is ground ahead of me. I am out of breath, panting, sweat trickling down my face in spite of a clamminess that persists on the back of my neck and shoulders. I hear movement behind me, turn, but see nothing.

I continue, driven, barely able to breathe. The manzanita clears, the ground levels further, and I pull myself into a patch of grass. I hear the rustle behind me again. This time I turn in time: there is a doe standing at the edge of the clearing, with twin fawns behind. I realize that these deer are the first living animals who've shown themselves to me all week, since the baby snake on the trail, even though the signs have told me there was wildlife all around. The doe stands calmly not ten feet from me. I am bent nearly in two, breathing heavily, covered with dirt and sweat, my hair awry. She looks directly into my wild and yearning eyes, as casually as if I were an old friend.

An unbelieving lightness comes over me. The weeks of loneliness and fear, of feeling like an exile in the natural world, dissolve in the unqualified acceptance of her steady, brown gaze. The lurking terror in my heart is gone. In its place is the certainty of abiding goodness, of God, and the knowledge of continuity beyond life and death.

Overwhelmed, I try to calm my trembling breath. Around me, the air seems to shimmer, and then suddenly life steps outside its masks. I am surrounded by Spirit. The physical forms — the bodies of the trees, the rocks, the deer, even myself — sublimate within the dazzling reality of eternal life.

And then I know — not believe, but *know* — that this body of mine will die some day. But I — the life that is in me — will continue to live, again and again, until finally that life is perfectly realized and I become one with God. The conviction of absolute, never-ending bliss runs through me like the blaze of a thousand suns.

I am no longer afraid. The exile imposed by my own spirit in ignorance is gone. The world takes the shape of the paradise of my dream; and now I, too, am part of it.

The lovely doe turns and bounds away into the manzanita, her fawns close at her heels. The brush hides them from my sight within seconds. Still quivering with emotion, I, too, turn to my path, and continue up the hill.

The climb is easier now, the slope more gradual, my steps, despite my shaky knees, more sure. I follow a deer path — different from the one that the doe and her fawns took — another 200 feet through manzanita, tall grass, and small oaks. Finally the earth turns horizontal: I am at the crest.

I pause, catch my breath, and try to determine where I am. Directly in front of me, to the west, is another ridge just like the one I'm on. After that one is another, and then another. Beyond many ridges, and two river forks, lies the ranch.

Turning back east, toward the sun, I find an opening in the brush from which I can see the river many feet below me. I rest and watch in a wordless and newfound knowledge of harmony with the world.

But I do not sit for long. I am suddenly eager to get on with life — the most immediate dilemma of which is descending this precipice without mishap. I know that going down will be at least as dangerous as going up.

I am more careful now, but the path is treacherous nonetheless. I slide and crawl, grabbing at convenient roots and limbs for support. I am not sure of the best route to take, but somehow it doesn't matter. I know that I will be all right.

My feet find their own way, and as I watch the velvet green of the river rise jerkily to meet me, a feeling of ecstasy dances within. The last hundred feet are the most difficult — but finally I am close enough to leap and then I am on the ground, at the river's edge. I kneel in the water, bathe my burning face, then peel off my clothes and dive deep and free into the cool, clear river.

The next morning I rise early to roll my sleeping bag, to gather my garbage to pack out, to try to erase the traces of my presence. I jump at the sound of a gunshot less than fifty feet away. The first person I have seen all week walks through the camp a moment later. "Just killed a rattler, ma'am, a big one, right by that big pool there." I shoulder my pack and start up the path toward home.

# XIV
# Even If Everyone Else
# Moved Away . . .

STRANGE how one season slides into the next. The tapping of the insects on my skylights trying to find a way out into the still-hot September air is so like the sound of winter rain that when I awake from an afternoon nap, I have to wonder when it is.

Fall is in the air as well as in my dreams; I smell it in the breeze, which has at last turned lively. But the rain is still some days or even weeks away. The meadow is parched, apparently stretched to the breaking point. Each new day that dawns clear and blue is borrowed time for the earth. I wonder how it can survive, how there can be any life still hiding within the hard, cracked soil. And yet I know that once the rains begin, little green shoots will poke their tips through even the most crusted of corners.

The river is quiet now, stained green by algae that thrive in its slow September waters. It winds lazily, fondling the rocks and curves as it passes, in no particular hurry. It is hard to believe that in two months it will be a swirling, muddy torrent, pushing over rocks and trees and bushes with impatience. Knowing that matter takes its form from spirit and that like attracts like, I can see that it is no accident that we have settled on land that is christened by this river. The river, with its unpredictable but stubbornly determined journey, remains the central image for our life here. Its course is neither short nor easy — often it flows in apparent contradiction to its goal — and yet it continues, never ceasing, from some mysterious source in the hills to the final unity, the sea.

What *is* the ranch, anyway? We have avoided defining it, even to each other, perhaps sensing that our definitions might not coincide. For me, it is the most perfect expression of my connection to nature that I can imagine. Even if everyone else moved away, this is where and how I would choose to live.

The political and social dimensions of what we are doing here are important to me. I believe in the true and honest quality of country life. In these confused and alienating times, it seems clear that the rural alternative must be a viable one, so that those who choose to do so can caretake (that is, take care of, nourish, and keep alive) the values that come from such direct experience with life and land.

Among those values are the understanding and respect for nature's laws that are fundamental to human survival. We on the ranch have just a little corner of the world to live with and, inadvertantly but inevitably, to experiment on. The sight of an overgrazed meadow or a clear-cut slope that can no longer support little trees is an effective lesson in the precise and delicate balance of nature. The same laws that govern here govern everywhere, though I know from my own experience that they are obscured in the city.

I also believe in the communal/collective social structure. Cumbersome as it may be at times, it seems a truer reflection of how life *is* — of how nature is — than the isolated individual existence that the modern city fosters. Autonomous units may still be more efficient in the short term, and therefore occasionally may be justified as a conscious choice of a way to do things, but it is foolish to forget that that independence is a conceptual illusion. Our lives are, in reality, deeply interdependent: ultimately, what is better for me must also be better for you; what hurts you hurts me as well. Yes, it is tedious to ask for a group consensus on whether or not to put in a new dam for the orchard irrigation, but as the world continues to shrink, as resources continue to diminish, the skills and the understanding that contribute to that consensus are more and more important to learning to live together on this planet.

But this doesn't mean that I think the world's problems would be solved if everyone packed up and moved to a commune in the country. No. The real problems are those of spirit, and the only true solutions will transpire within the intimacy of each one's relation to God, as they have throughout time. The political and social dimensions of what we are doing here are important to me — but they are afterthoughts, coincidental to the fabric of day-to-day life. That fabric results from the compulsion to live true, responsible individual lives, regardless of the social or political implications. The ranch is the product of that compulsion and of what appears to be our overlapping individual destinies; I doubt that it would work on any other basis. But the same inner laws which have brought us here must guide others elsewhere.

The land for me is what dreams were for Jung, what numbers were for Pythagoras. It is my window into a larger reality.

I remember the first time in this life that I began to suspect that things might not be quite as they seem, that there might be more to reality than the simple here and now. With that suspicion came the sensation of the bottom dropping out.

I was nine and it was time to tell me about the changes my little girl's body was about to go through. I was fortunate at having somehow escaped the back-fence vehicle of information that puts a permanent dirty feeling on the wondrous process of growing up for so many young girls. It was a hot summer day. My mother made us each a glass of lemonade and we sat together on the back screened porch. It was not a particularly unusual thing for us to do, but I remember knowing somehow that this was not going to be just another glass of lemonade. "Do you know what menstruation is?" my mother asked.

Right then it started, the curious sense of being both old and young, of digging deep for where I did know, of feeling the bottom drop from my nine-year-old existence and merge someplace with a far older, wiser me. Age-old me woke up and, from a distance, watched my nine-year-old self respond after a moment's hesitation, "Hmmm . . . anything to do with men?" My mother laughed, no doubt relieved by my obvious innocence, happy not to have to combat strange half-truths which might have been passed to me by less reputable channels. And she went on to tell me what somewhere I already knew, about the magic of becoming a woman.

I was not so lucky in learning the true story of how babies are made. That was the back-fence version ("He does *what*?"), no doubt slightly off-key from my mother's version (which, when she tried to tell me a year or two later, I haughtily informed her I had no need of, since I already knew it all). But it, too, was accompanied by the same vertigo, the same dizzying sensation of suddenly bringing to light something that part of me already knew.

It happens often here: I watch a hawk soar through the morning sky and something falls into place within me. It is as if I travel through a wood long unvisited and recognize familiar trees grown taller with the passing of time. I come upon a thought, an act, a place with the vague sense of having thought that, done that, been there once before. Or I come to a fork in the road and I know by some unexplainable sense which is right for me. I walk and uncover or discover anew what I have always known.

Living intimately with nature opens doors in my spirit; the mystery becomes known, darkness becomes light. The land comforts me, nourishes me — but above all, enlarges my reality and leads me unerringly where I want to go.

The vultures once again fly patterns in the evening sky. The temperature drops low after sundown, and in the early morning there is a thin film of dew on the meadow. Autumn approaches: our sixth. My wood is not yet in; there are tomatoes to can before it frosts; I have not yet replaced my raincoat of many seasons, now in tatters and not fit for even a timid shower. I wonder how the yurt will weather yet another round of winter; I should have a skylight replacement at hand. I have a fleeting moment of concern: there seems so much to do, the season is changing too fast: I am not ready. How will I ever be able to do it?

The feeling catches on something and I am suddenly back in third grade listening to Dan Robertson worry about whether or not he will be able to do fourth grade work. Multiplication and long division seem like insurmountable obstacles from his third grade perspective. He talks to me for days, then weeks, and finally I begin to worry, too. Then one day a smile replaces his worry lines. He tells me about it at recess.

His mother, concerned over her eight-year-old son who seemed to be carrying the weight of middle age, had finally pried open his fear the night before. He confessed to her that he was terrified that he wouldn't be able to make it in fourth grade. With a dramatic pause, he looks me in the eye for the first time in many a week. "And you know what she said?" he says triumphantly. "She said I shouldn't worry. She said that by the time I get to fourth grade I will be able to do the work. She said that that is what third grade is all about."

I remember that now, that child's version of the wisdom of the ages: live each moment fully, do your task at hand, and you will also be able to do the next.

My perspective restored, I go out into the fading light to watch the sun shine golden on the vultures' wings. Round and round they fly, and I feel a corresponding turning somewhere within. My seasons, too, are changing, weaving in and out of one another in patterns too broad for my eye to see. I feel a tingling fullness around these September days.

The sun and shadow weave black and gold tapestry on the evening sky. As I watch, time suspends itself, and this moment falls into a pool of eternity, sending sympathetic ripples both forward and backward in rich and ever-widening circles. The sun settles gently behind the western hills. I am at peace.

DESIGN AND MECHANICALS BY DIANA FAIRBANKS.

TITLES SET IN UNIVERSITY OF CALIFORNIA OLD STYLE, A TYPE DESIGNED

BY FREDERIC W. GOUDY IN 1940 FOR THE UNIVERSITY OF CALIFORNIA PRESS

ON THE 500TH ANNIVERSARY OF GUTENBERG'S MOVABLE TYPE;

BY HAND AT THE YOLLA BOLLY PRESS, COVELO, CALIFORNIA.

TEXT TYPE SET IN BASKERVILLE BY SHEILA SINGLETON

AT THE ROUND VALLEY NEWS, COVELO, CALIFORNIA.

PRINTED ON 60 POUND WARREN'S OLD STYLE AND PERFECT BOUND

BY THOMSON-SHORE, DEXTER, MICHIGAN.